كتاب شكرستان
در نحوي زبان پارسي
تصنيف يونس اوكسفردي

A GRAMMAR OF THE PERSIAN LANGUAGE.

BY SIR WILLIAM JONES,

OF UNIVERSITY COLLEGE, OXFORD, AND OF THE ROYAL SOCIETIES OF LONDON AND COPENHAGEN.

چو عندليب فصاحت فروشد اي حافظ
تو قدر او بسخن گفتن دري بشكن

KITAB BHAVAN
Publishers, Distributors, Exporters & Importers

Grammer of the Persian 2017

KITAB BHAVAN
Publishers, Distributors, Exporters & Importers
1784, Kalan Mahal, Darya Ganj,
New Delhi - 1100 02 (India)
Phones : (91-11) 23277392 / 93, 23274686
Fax : (91-11) 23263383

Online Store: www.kitabbavan.net

Email : info@kitabbhavan.net
: nasri@vsnl.com

First Published : 1809
Reprint : 2017

ISBN : 978-81-9335-7323
Book Code No. : G00045

Printed & Published in India by :
Nusrat Ali Nasri for KITAB BHAVAN
Moonis Ali Nasri for KITAB BHAVAN
1784, Kalan Mahal, Darya Ganj,
New Delhi - 1100 02 [India]

CONTENTS

THE

PREFACE.

THE Persian language is rich, melodious, and elegant; it has been spoken for many ages by the greatest princes in the politest courts of Asia; and a number of admirable works have been written in it by historians, philosophers, and poets, who found it capable of expressing with equal advantage the most beautiful and the most elevated sentiments.

It must seem strange, therefore, that the study of this language should be so little cultivated at a time when a taste for general and diffusive learning seems universally to prevail; and that the fine productions of a celebrated nation should remain in manuscript upon the shelves of our public libraries, without a single admirer who might open their treasures to his countrymen, and display their beauties to the light; but if we consider the subject with a proper attention, we shall discover a variety of causes which have concurred to obstruct the progress of Eastern literature.

Some men never heard of the Asiatic writings, and others will not be convinced that there is any thing valuable in them; some pretend to be busy, and others are really idle; some detest the Persians, because they believe in Mahomed, and others despise their language because they do not understand it: we all love to excuse, or to conceal, our ignorance, and are seldom willing to allow any excellence beyond the limits of our own attainments; like the savages who thought that the sun rose and set for them alone, and could not imagine that the waves, which surrounded their island, left coral and pearls upon any other shore.

Another obvious reason for the neglect of the Persian language is the great scarcity of books, which are necessary to be read before it can be perfectly learned, the greater part of them are preserved in the different museums and libraries of Europe, where they are shewn more as objects of curiosity than as sources of information; and are admired, like the characters on a Chinese screen, more for their gay colours than for their meaning.

Thus, while the excellent writings of Greece and Rome are studied by every man of a liberal education, and diffuse a general refinement through our part of the world, the works of the Persians, a nation equally distinguished in ancient history, are either wholly unknown to us, or considered as entirely destitute of taste and invention.

But if this branch of literature has met with so many obstructions from the ignorant, it has, certainly, been checked in its progress by the learned themselves; most of whom have confined their study to the minute researches of verbal criticism; like men who discover a precious mine, but instead of searching for the rich ore, or for gems, amuse themselves with collecting smooth pebbles and pieces of crystal. Others mistook reading for learning, which ought to be carefully distinguished by every man of sense, and were satisfied with running over a great number of manuscripts in a superficial manner, without condescending to be stopped by their difficulty, or to dwell upon their beauty and elegance. The rest have left nothing more behind them than grammars and dictionaries; and though they deserve the praises due to unwearied pains and industry, yet they would, perhaps, have gained a more shining reputation, if they had contributed to beautify and enlighten the vast temple of learning, instead of spending their lives in adorning only its porticos and avenues.

There is nothing which has tended more to bring polite letters into discredit, than the total insensibility of commentators and critics to the beauties of the authors whom they profess to illustrate: few of them seem to have received the smallest pleasure from the most elegant compositions, unless they found some mistake of a transcriber to be corrected, or some established reading to be changed, some obscure expression to be explained, or some clear passage to be made obscure by their notes.

It is a circumstance equally unfortunate that men of the most refined taste and the brightest parts are apt to look upon a close application to the study of languages as inconsistent with their spirit and genius: so that the state of letters seems to be divided into two classes, men of learning who have no taste, and men of taste who have no learning.

M. de Voltaire, who excels all writers of his age and country in the elegance of his style, and the wonderful variety of his talents, acknowledges the beauty of the Persian images and sentiments, and has versified a fine passage from Sadi, whom he compares to Petrarch: if that extraordinary man had added a knowledge of the Asiatic languages to his other acquisitions, we should by this time have seen the poems and histories of Persia in an European dress, and any other recommendation of them would have been unnecessary.

But there is yet another cause which has operated more strongly than any before mentioned towards preventing the rise of Oriental literature; I mean the small encouragement which the princes and nobles of Europe have given to men of letters. It is an indisputable truth, that learning will always flourish most where the amplest rewards are proposed to the industry of the learned; and that the most shining periods in the annals of literature are the reigns of wise and liberal princes, who know that fine writers are the oracles of the world, from whose testimony every king, statesman, and hero must expect the censure or approbation of posterity. In the old states of Greece the highest honours were given to poets, philosophers and orators; and a single city (as an eminent writer* observes) in the

* Ascham.

memory of one man, produced more numerous and splendid monuments of human genius than most other nations have afforded in a course of ages.

The liberality of the Ptolemies in Egypt drew a number of learned men and poets to their court, whose works remain to the present age the models of taste and elegance; and the writers, whom Augustus protected, brought their compositions to a degree of perfection, which the language of mortals cannot surpass. Whilst all the nations of Europe were covered with the deepest shade of ignorance, the Califs in Asia encouraged the Mahomedans to improve their talents, and cultivate the fine arts; and even the Turkish Sultan, who drove the Greeks from Constantinople, was a patron of literary merit, and was himself an elegant poet. The illustrious family of Medici invited to Florence the learned men whom the Turks had driven from their country; and a general light succeeded to the gloom which ignorance and superstition had spread through the western world. But that light has not continued to shine with equal splendour; and though some slight efforts have been made to restore it, yet it seems to have been gradually decaying for the last century: it grows very faint in Italy;

it seems wholly extinguished in France, and whatever sparks of it remain in other countries are confined to the closets of humble and modest men, and are not general enough to have their proper influence.

The nobles of our days consider learning as a subordinate acquisition, which would not be consistent with the dignity of their fortunes, and should be left to those who toil in a lower sphere of life; but they do not reflect on the many advantages which the study of polite letters would give peculiarly to persons of eminent rank and high employments; who, instead of relieving their fatigues by a series of unmanly pleasures, or useless diversions, might spend their leisure in improving their knowledge, and in conversing with the great statesmen, orators, and philosophers of antiquity.

If learning in general has met with so little encouragement, still less can be expected for that branch of it, which lies so far removed from the common path, and which the greater part of mankind have hitherto considered as incapable of yielding either entertainment or instruction: if pains and want be the lot of a scholar, the life of an Orientalist must certainly be attended with peculiar hardships.

Gentius, who published a beautiful Persian work called *the Bed of Roses*, with an useful but inelegant translation, lived obscurely in Holland, and died in misery. Hyde, who might have contributed greatly towards the progress of Eastern learning, formed a number of expensive projects with that view, but had not the support and assistance which they deserved and required. The labours of Meninski immortalized and ruined him: his Dictionary of the Asiatic language is perhaps, the most laborious compilation that was ever undertaken by any single man; but he complains in his preface that his patrimony was exhausted by the great expense of employing and supporting a number of writers and printers, and of raising a new press for the Oriental characters. M. d'Herbelot, indeed, received the most splendid reward of his industry: he was invited to Italy by Ferdinand II. Duke of Tuscany, who entertained him with that striking munificence which always distinguished the race of the Medici: after the death of Ferdinand, the illustrious Colbert recalled him to Paris, where he enjoyed the fruits of his labour, and spent the remainder of his days in an honourable and easy retirement. But this is a rare example: the other princes of Europe have not imitated the Duke of Tuscany; and Christian VII. was reserved to be the protector of the Eastern Muses in the present age.

Since the literature of Asia was so much neglected, and the causes of that neglect were so various, we could not have expected that any slight power would rouse the nations of Europe from their inattention to it; and they would, perhaps, have persisted in despising it, if they had not been animated by the most powerful incentive that can influence the mind of man: interest was the magic wand which brought them all within one circle; interest was the charm which gave the languages of the East a real and solid importance. By one of those revolutions, which no human prudence could have foreseen, the Persian language found its way into India; that rich and celebrated empire, which, by the flourishing state of our commerce, has been the source of incredible wealth to the merchants of Europe. A variety of causes, which need not be mentioned here, gave the English nation a most extensive power in that kingdom: our India Company began to take under their protection the princes of the country, by whose protection they gained their first settlement; a number of important affairs were to be transacted in peace and war between nations equally jealous of one another, who had not the common instrument of conveying their sentiments; the servants of the company received letters which they could not read, and were ambitious of gaining titles of which they could not comprehend the meaning; it was found highly dangerous to employ the natives as interpreters, upon whose fidelity they could not depend; and it was at last discovered, that they must apply themselves to the study of the Persian language, in which all the letters from the Indian princes were written. A few men of parts and taste, who resided in Bengal, have since amused themselves with the literature of the East, and have spent their leisure in reading the poems and histories of Persia; but they found a reason in every page to regret their ignorance of the Arabic language, without which their knowledge must be very circumscribed and imperfect. The languages of Asia will now, perhaps, be studied with uncommon ardour; they are known to be useful, and will soon be found instructive and entertaining; the valuable manuscripts that enrich our public libraries will be in a few years elegantly printed; the manners and sentiments of the Eastern nations will be perfectly known;

and the limits of our knowledge will be no less extended than the bounds of our empire.

It was with a view to facilitate the progress of this branch of literature, that I reduced to order the following instructions for the Persian language which I had collected several years ago; but I would not present my grammar to the public till I had considerably enlarged and improved it: I have, therefore, endeavoured to lay down the clearest and most accurate rules, which I have illustrated by select examples from the most elegant writers; I have carefully compared my work with every composition of the same nature that has fallen into my hands; and though on so general a subject I must have made several observations which are common to all, yet I flatter myself that my own remarks, the disposition of the whole book, and the passages quoted in it, will sufficiently distinguish it as an original production. Though I am not conscious that there are any essential mistakes or omissions in it, yet I am sensible that it falls very short of perfection, which seems to withdraw itself from the pursuit of mortals, in proportion to their endeavours of attaining it; like the talisman in the Arabian tales, which a bird carried from tree to tree as often as its pursuer approached it. But it has been my chief care to avoid all the harsh and affected terms of art which render most didactic works so tedious and unpleasant, and which only perplex the learner, without giving him any real knowledge: I have even refrained from making any inquiries into general grammar, or from entering into those subjects which have already been so elegantly discussed by the most judicious philosopher,* the most learned divine,† and the most laborious scholar of the present age.‡

It was my first design to prefix to the grammar a history of the Persian language from the time of Xenophon to our days, and to have added a copious praxis of tales and poems extracted from the classical writers of Persia; but as those additions would have delayed the publication of the grammar, which was principally wanted, I thought it advisable to reserve them for a separate volume, which the public may expect in the course of the ensuing winter. I have made a large collection of materials for a general history of Asia, and for an account of the geography, phi-

* See Hermes. † A short Introduction to English Grammar.

‡ See grammar prefixed to the Dictionary of the English Language.

losophy, and literature of the Eastern nations, all which I propose to arrange in order, if my more solid and more important studies will allow me any intervals of leisure.*

I cannot forbear acknowledging in this place the signal marks of kindness and attention, which I have received from many learned and noble persons; but General Carnac has obliged me the most sensibly of them, by supplying me with a valuable collection of Persian manuscripts on every branch of Eastern learning, from which many of the best examples in the following grammar are extracted. A very learned Professor † at Oxford has promoted my studies with that candour and benevolence which so eminently distinguish him; and many excellent men that are the principal ornaments of that University have conferred the highest favours on me, of which I shall ever retain a grateful sense: but I take a singular pleasure in confessing that I am indebted to a foreign nobleman ‡ for the little knowledge which I have happened to acquire of the Persian language; and that my zeal for the poetry and philology of

* See the *History of the Persian Language* a *Description of Asia*, and a *Short History of Persia*, published with my *Life of Nader Shah* in the year 1773.

† Dr. Hunt.

‡ Baron Reviski.

the Asiatics, was owing to his conversation, and to the agreeable correspondence with which he still honours me.

Before I conclude this preface, it will be proper to add a few remarks upon the method of learning the Persian language, and upon the advantages which the learner may expect from it. When the student can read the characters with fluency, and has learned the true pronunciation of every letter from the mouth of a native, let him peruse the grammar with attention, and commit to memory the regular inflexions of the nouns and verbs: he need not burden his mind with those that deviate from the common form, as they will be insensibly learned in a short course of reading. By this time he will find a dictionary necessary, and I hope he will believe me, when I assert from a long experience, that, whoever possesses the admirable work of Meninski,* will have no occasion for any other dictionary of the Persian tongue. He may proceed by the help of this work to analyse the passages quoted in the grammar, and to examine in what manner they illustrate the rules: in the mean time he must not neglect to converse with his living instructor, and to learn from him the phrases of

* This was written before Richardson's Dictionary was published.

common discourse, and the names of visible objects, which he will soon imprint on his memory, if he will take the trouble to look for them in the dictionary; and here I must caution him against condemning a work as defective, because he cannot find in it every word which he hears: for sounds in general are caught imperfectly by the ear, and many words are spelt and pronounced very differently.

The first book that I would recommend to him is the Gulistán, or *Bed of Roses*, a work which is highly esteemed in the East, and of which there are several translations in the languages of Europe: the manuscripts of this book are very common; and by comparing them with the printed edition of Gentius, he will soon learn the beautiful flowing hand used in Persia, which consists of bold strokes and flourishes, and cannot be imitated by our types. It will then be a proper time for him to read some short and easy chapter in this work, and to translate it into his native language with the utmost exactness; let him then lay aside the original, and after a proper interval let him turn the same chapter back into Persian by the assistance of the grammar and dictionary: let him afterwards compare his second translation with the original, and correct its faults according to that model. This is the exercise so often recommended by the old rhetoricians, by which a student will gradually acquire the style and manner of any author, whom he desires to imitate, and by which almost any language may be learned in six months with ease and pleasure. When he can express his sentiments in Persian with tolerable facility, I would advise him to read some elegant history or poem with an intelligent native, who will explain to him in common words the refined expressions that occur in reading, and will point out the beauties of learned allusions and local images. The most excellent book in the language is, in my opinion, the collection of tales and fables called *Anver Soheili* by Hussein Vaés, surnamed Cashefi, who took the celebrated work of Bidpai or Pilpay for his text, and has comprised all the wisdom of the Eastern nations, in fourteen beautiful chapters. At some leisure hour he may desire his Munshi or writer to transcribe a section from the Gulistán, or a fable of Cashefi, in the common broken hand used in India, which he will learn perfectly in a few days by comparing all its turns and contractions with the more regular hands of the Arabs and Persians: he must not be discouraged by the difficulty of reading the Indian letters, for the characters are in reality the same with those in which our books are printed, and are only rendered difficult by the frequent omission of the diacritical points, and the want of regularity in the position of the words: but we all know that we are often at a loss to read letters which we receive in our native tongue; and it has been proved that a man who has a perfect knowledge of any language, may with a proper attention decypher a letter in that idiom, though it be written in characters which he has never seen before, and of which he has no alphabet.

In short, I am persuaded that whoever will study the Persian language according to my plan, will in less than a year be able to translate and to answer any letter from an Indian prince, and to converse with the natives of India, not only with fluency, but with elegance. But if he desires to distinguish himself as an eminent translator, and to understand not only the general purport of a composition, but even the graces and ornaments of it, he must necessarily learn the Arabic tongue, which is blended with the Persian in so singular a manner, that one period often contains both languages wholly distinct from each other in expression and idiom, but perfectly united in sense and construction. This must appear strange to an European reader; but he may form some idea of this uncommon mixture, when he is told that the two Asiatic languages are not always mixed like the words of Roman and Saxon origin in this period, "The true law is right reason, conformable "to the nature of things, which calls us to duty by com- "manding, deters us from sin by forbidding;*" but as we may suppose the Latin and English to be connected in the following sentence; "*The true* lex *is* recta ratio, *conformable* naturæ, *which by commanding* vocet ad officium, *by forbidding* à fraude deterreat."

A knowledge of these two languages will be attended with a variety of advantages to those who acquire it: the Hebrew, Chaldaic, Syriac, and Ethiopian tongues, are dialects of the Arabic, and bear as near a resemblance to it as the Ionic to the Attic Greek; the jargon of Indostan, very improperly called the language of the Moors, contains so great a number of Persian words, that I was able, with

* See Middleton's Life of Cicero, vol. III. p. 351.

very little difficulty, to read the fables of Pilpai which are translated into that idiom; the Turkish contains ten Arabic or Persian words for one originally Scythian, by which it has been so refined that the modern kings of Persia were fond of speaking it in their courts: in short, there is scarce a country in Asia or Africa, from the source of the Nile to the wall of China, in which a man who understands Arabic, Persian, and Turkish, may not travel with satisfaction, or transact the most important affairs with advantage and security.

As to the literature of Asia, it will not, perhaps, be essentially useful to the greater part of mankind, who have neither leisure nor inclination to cultivate so extensive a branch of learning; but the civil and natural history of such mighty empires as India, Persia, Arabia, and Tartary, cannot fail of delighting those who love to view the great picture of the universe, or to learn by what degrees the most obscure states have risen to glory, and the most flourishing kingdoms have sunk to decay; the philosopher will consider those works as highly valuable, by which he may trace the human mind in all its various appearances, from the rudest to the most cultivated state: and the man of taste will undoubtedly be pleased to unlock the stores of native genius, and to gather the flowers of unrestrained and luxuriant fancy.*

* Note to the Third Edition.

My professional studies having wholly engaged my attention, and induced me not only to abandon Oriental literature, but even to efface, as far as possible, the very traces of it from my memory, I committed the conduct and revisal of this edition of my grammar, and the composition of the index, to Mr. Richardson, in whose skill I have a perfect confidence, and from whose application to the Eastern languages, I have hopes that the learned world will reap no small advantage.

ADVERTISEMENT.

In presenting this the sixth edition of Sir William Jones's inestimable Persian Grammar to the Public, the Editor thinks proper to apprize his readers of such improvements and alterations as he has found it expedient to make therein

The work has been carefully revised, and many errors which had been accumulating with every former edition, have been attentively corrected.

Great improvement has been made in the printing and paper; and it comes forth with an elegant new type, cut after the best examples of writing in the Niskhi *character, and of which no specimen has before been published.*

Some examples in Prose, designed for the exercise of

the student, have been added, printed in types of two sizes, both entirely new.

The Editors of Richardson's Persian and Arabic Dictionary, (as will more fully appear from the notice subjoined to this work), having caused great alterations, with numerous additions and improvements, to be made in the new and more convenient form it is about to assume; and being of opinion that this Grammar, as a necessary companion, should be made to correspond with it, the same mode of spelling the Persian words in Roman characters has herein been adopted, as is pursuing in the revision of that Dictionary; and which being upon a plan at once both regular and simple, cannot, we think, but be of great use to beginners in particular, as an invariable guide to the pronunciation. The plan is developed in the body of this work in its proper place, the part which treats on the power of the letters. At the time the learned author of this truly elegant and useful Grammar composed it, he does not seem to have formed that system of orthography of Asiatic words in Roman letters which he afterwards so ably explains in the opening of the first Volume of the Asiatic

Researches, else but little occasion would have been found for the alterations it has been judged expedient to make.

THE EDITOR.

N. B. The Improvements pointed out in the foregoing Advertisement to the Sixth Edition of this Work, have been continued in the present.

وجود کردن to commit, perform, give a being to.	هرجا که whenever.
وار or ور like, possessing.	هرچه or هرانچه whatsoever.
ورق A. a leaf *of a* tree *or* paper.	هرچند or هرچندکه although.
وز and from.	هرکجا wherever.
وزید it blows. *from* وزیدن	هرکجاکه wheresoever.
وست he, she, it is.	هرگز ever.
وش like, resembling.	هرگزنه never.
وصال A. enjoyment; arrival; meeting; conjunction.	هرکه or هرانکه whosoever.
	هزار a thousand; a nightingale.
	هستن to be, exist.

كتاب
شكرستان
درنحوي زبان پارسي

A GRAMMAR OF THE PERSIAN LANGUAGE.

OF LETTERS.

THE learner is supposed to be acquainted with the common terms of grammar, and to know that the Persians write their characters from the right hand to the left.

There are thirty-two Persian letters.

	IV.	III.	II.	I.	
	FINALS.		INITIALS and MEDIALS.		
	Connected.	Unconnected	Connected.	Unconnected.	
alif	ـا	ا	ـا	ا	a
bē	ـب	ب	ـبـ ـبـ	بـ	b
pē	ـپ	پ	ـپـ ـپـ	پـ	p
tē	ـت	ت	ـتـ ـتـ	تـ	ṭ
sē	ـث	ث	ـثـ ـثـ	ثـ	ṣ
jīm	ـج	ج	ـجـ	جـ	j English
chē or chīm	ـچ	چ	ـچـ	چـ	ch
hē	ـح	ح	ـحـ	حـ	ḥ strong
khē	ـخ	خ	ـخـ	خـ	kh
dāl	ـد	د	ـد	د	d
zāl	ـذ	ذ	ـذ	ذ	ż
rē	ـر	ر	ـر	ر	r
zē	ـز	ز	ـز	ز	z̈
zhē	ـژ	ژ	ـژ	ژ	j French
sīn	ـس	س	ـسـ	سـ	s̱
shīn	ـش	ش	ـشـ	شـ	sh
swād	ـص	ص	ـصـ	صـ	ṣ
zwād	ـض	ض	ـضـ	ضـ	ż
tō	ـط	ط	ـطـ	طـ	ṭ

	IV.	III.	II.	I.	
	FINALS.		INITIALS and MEDIALS.		
	Connected.	Unconnected.	Connected.	Unconnected.	
zō	ـظ	ظ	ـظـ	ظـ	z̈
ain	ـع	ع	ـعـ	عـ	ع or *a* guttural
ghain	ـغ	غ	ـغـ	غـ	gh guttural
fē	ـف	ف	ـفـ	فـ	f
kāf	ـق	ق	ـقـ	قـ	ḳ hard
cāf	ـک	ک	ـکـ ـکـ or	کـ	k̦
gāf	ـگ	گ	ـگـ	گـ	g hard
lām	ـل	ل	ـلـ	لـ	l
mīm	ـم	م	ـمـ ـمـ	مـ	m
nun	ـن	ن	ـنـ	نـ	n
wāw	ـو	و	ـو	و	u, v, w
hē	ـه	ه	ـهـ	هـ	ḥ weak
yā	ـي	ي	ـيـ	يـ	y, ī
lām-alif	ـلا	لا	ـلا	لا	lā

The second and fourth columns of these letters from the right hand are used only when they are connected with a preceding letter; as محمد Muhammad. Every letter should be connected with that which follows it, except these seven; ا alif, د dāl, ذ zāl, ر rē, ز zē, ژ jē and و wāw, which are never joined to the following letter, as will appear from the words برگ barg, *a leaf*, داوري dāvarī, *a dominion*.

Though the perfect pronunciation of these letters can be learned only from the mouth of a Persian or an Indian, yet it will be proper to add a few observations upon the most remarkable of them.

OF CONSONANTS.

It will be needless to say much of the three first consonants ب پ ت since their sound is exactly the same as our *b*, *p*, and *t*, in the words *bar*, *peer*, and *too*, which would be written in Persian بار پير and تو.

ث ṣ.

This letter, which the Arabs pronounce somewhat like a *th*, has in Persian the same sound with a س or *s*, as ابوليث Abū Lays, a proper name. It might, therefore, have been rejected from the Persian alphabet without any inconvenience; but it is useful in showing the origin of words, as it is seldom, or never, used in any that are not Arabic. The same may be observed of the following letters, ق غ ع ظ ط ض ص ح which rarely occur in words originally Persian.

ج j and چ ch

The first of these letters answers to our soft *g* in *gem*, which a Persian would write جم, or to our *j* in *jar* جار; the second of them چ sounds exactly like our *ch* in the words *cherry, cheek;* as چرکس Chirkas, *Circassia.*

ح ḥ

ح is a very strong aspirate, and may be expressed in our characters by ḥ (with a dot under it to distinguish it from ه), as حال ḥāl, a *condition.*

خ kh

خ is formed in the throat (and produces that kind of inarticulate vibration which is made in preparing to expectorate). The Germans have the sound, and express it by *ch.* The sound does not exist in English; and having no simple character for it, we use *kh* as its substitute: as خان khān, *a lord.* This is the word so variously and so erroneously written by the Europeans. The sovereign lord of Tartary is neither the *cham*, as our travellers call him, nor the *han*, as Voltaire will have it, but the خان khān, with a guttural aspirate on the first letter.

د d

د answers exactly to our *d* in *deer* دیر

ذ ż

This letter, which the Arabs pronounce somewhat like *dh*, has in Persian the sound of ز ż, and is often confounded with it; thus they write گذشتن and گزشتن guźishṭan, *to pass*: It is seldom used but in Arabick words; though it sometimes occurs in words purely Persian, as اذربیجان Ażarbījān, *the province of Media*, so called from اذر ażar, an old word for *fire*, because the adorers of fire, if we believe the Asiatick historians, first built their temples in that province.

ر r

ر and the three liquids ل م ن are pronounced exactly like our *r*, *l*, *m*, *n*; as آرام ārām, *rest*, لاله lālah, *a tulip*, مار mār, *a serpent*, نان nān, *bread*. But ن before a ب

has the sound of *m*, as گنبد gumbad, *a tower*, عنبر ꞔamber, *ambergris*.

ز z

has the sound of our *z*, as لالهزار lālahẑār, *a bed of tulips.*

ژ j̈

This letter has the sound of our *s* in the word *pleasure*, *treasure;* and corresponds precisely with the soft *g* of the French in *gens*, or their *j* in *jour*. It may be expressed in our characters by j̈ with two dots, as ژاله j̈ālah, *dew*.

س s ش sh

س and ش are our *s* and *sh*, as سليم شاه ṣalīm shāh, *king Selim.*

ص ṣ ض ẑ ط ṭ ظ z̈

These four letters are pronounced by the Arabs in a manner peculiar to themselves; but in Persian they are confounded with other letters. ص differs little from س as صددر ṣaddar, *the name of a Persian book;* and ط has nearly the same sound with ت as عطر ꞔaṭr, *essence;* a word often used in English, since our connexion with India, to denote the precious perfume called *otter of roses.* The word is Arabic, as the letters ع and ط sufficiently prove. ض and ظ differ very little from ز; as نظامي Nažāmī, *the name of a poet;* خضر Khažar, *the name of a prophet in the Eastern romances.*

ع ع and غ gh

These two letters are extremely harsh in the pronunciation of the Arabs. The sound of ع, says Meninski, *est vox vituli matrem vocantis.* (It is considered as a consonant, and occasions any vowel, with which it is connected, to be pronounced as if from the chest; but as no letters can convey an idea of its force, in imitation of Meninski, we have used the Arabic form in combination with the Roman and Italic characters), as in the word عرب ع‍arab, *the Arabians;* عين ع‍ayn, *a fountain.* As to غ it is pronounced something like our hard *gh* in the word *ghost*, as غلام ghulām, *a boy, a servant.* (The true sound of غ is that which is produced in gargling).

ف f

ف has the sound of *f* in *fall*, as فال fāl, *an omen.*

ق ḳand ك k

ق is another harsh Arabic letter, but in Persian it is often confounded with ك, which has the sound of our *k*, a كرمان Karmān, *the province of Carmania;* قاف Ḳāf, *a fabulous mountain in the Oriental tales.*

گ g

When ك has a small stroke over its upper member, or three points above it, the Persians give it the sound of *g* in the word *gay*, as گلستان gulistān, *a bed of roses;* but these marks are very seldom written in the Persian manuscripts; so that the distinction between ك k and گ g can be learned only by use: thus they often write كلاب *rose water*, and pronounce it gulāb. (The letter g, without any mark, is its natural representative).

ل م ن

See the remark on ر. These letters are the liquids *l, m, n, r.*

ه h

ه is a slight aspiration, as in بهار bahār, *the spring*, هرات Harāt, *a city in the province of Corasan*, which the

Greeks call Aria. At the end of a Persian word it generally serves only to shew that it terminates in a vowel, as كه keh̤, which has the same pronunciation as the Italian *che*, what. (It may in European characters be represented by h̤ with two dots, to distinguish it from ح ḥ. (Observe that when this character has two dots over it thus ة it is pronounced as ت ṭ).

OF VOWELS.

The vowels are ا a, و u, ي i, as in the words خان khān, *a lord*, اورا ōrā, *to him*, نيز nīz, *also*, where they are all long; but the short vowels are expressed by small marks, two of which are placed above the letter, and one below it, as بَ bă, بِ bĕ or bĭ, بُ bŏ or bŭ: thus,

اگَر آن تُرْکِ شِیرازِي بَدَسْت آرَد دِلِ مارا
بَخالِ هِنْدُوِیش بَخْشَم سَمَرقَنْد وَبُخارارا

Agar ān ṭurki Shīrāzī badasṭ ārad dili mārā
Bakhāli hindūyash bakhsham Samarḳand wa Bokhārārā.

(*Note.* ا alif, at the beginning of a word, not being distinguished by the mark *mad* over it, thus آ, is not only always short, but occasionally pronounced as the short vowels ă, ĭ, ŭ. In the middle or at the end of a word it is generally long by position, though it have no mark over it).

The mark ْ placed above a consonant shows that the syllable ends with it, as سَمَرْقَنْدِي Sa-mar-kan-dī, *a native of Samarcand;* the first of which syllables is short, the second and third long by position, and the last long by nature: but this belongs to the prosody. These short vowels are very seldom written in the Persian books: and the other orthographical marks are likewise usually suppressed, except Medda ~, Hamza ء and Teshdid ّ.

Medda above an ا gives it a broad and long sound (like two alifs), as آن ān, *that;* Hamza (with the mark of short ĭ expressed or understood, and placed at the foot of the letter) supplies the place of ي in words that end in ه; it therefore sometimes represents the article, as نامهٔ nāmahi, *a book;* or denotes the former of two substantives, as نافهٔ مشک nāfahi mushk, *a bag of musk;* or, lastly, it occasionally marks the second person singular in the compound preterite of a verb, as داده‌ dādahi, which would regularly be داده‌ اي, *thou hast given.* Tashdid shews a consonant to be doubled, as طرّه turrah, *a lock of hair.*

The omission of the short vowels will at first perplex the student; since many words, that are compounded of the same letters, have different senses, according to the difference of the vowels omitted: but until he has learned the exact pronunciation of every word from a native, he may give every short vowel a kind of obscure sound very common in English, as in the words *sun, bird, mother,* which a Mahometan would write without any vowel, *sn, brd, mthr;* thus the Persian word بد bd may be pronounced like our *bud* (This short obscure sound in the words *sun, bird, &c.* is the exact power which those who speak the Persian language in India give to the short vowel called *Fatah,* and which it is convenient to represent by *a.* In this edition the short vowels are represented by *a* for ´, *i* and sometimes *e* for , and *u* and occasionally *o* for ʼ; and the long vowels are distinguished from the short by the prosodial mark of a long syllable, thus ā, ī, ē, ō, ū).

Wāw و and Yā ي are often used as consonants, like our *w* and *y*; thus وان Wān, *a town in Armenia;* جوان jawān *juvenis, giovane,* young; يمن Yaman, that province of Arabia which we call *the happy;* خدايار Khudāyār a proper name, signifying *the friend of God.* و before ا often loses its sound, as خوان kh'ān, *a table.* (و, when considered as a consonant, has a sound somewhat between *w* and *v*).

I would not advise the learner to study the parts of speech until he can read the Persian characters with tolerable fluency; which he will soon be able to do, if he will spend a few hours in writing a page or two of Persian in English letters (following the system of orthography used in the following example), and restoring them after a short interval to their proper characters by the help of the alphabet. I shall close this section with a piece of Persian poetry written both in the Asiatick and European characters: it is an ode by the poet Hafiz, the first couplet of which has been already quoted; and a translation of it shall be inserted in its proper place.

بده ساقي مي باقي كه در جنّت نخواهي يافت
كنار آب ركناباد و گلگشت مصلّارا

Badeḥ sāḳī may-i bāḳī keḥ dar jannaṭ nakh'āḥī yāfṭ,
Ḳanār-i āb-i ruḳnābād wa gulgashṭ-i muṣallārā.

فغان كين لوليان شوخ شيرينگار شهر آشوب
چنان بردند صبر از دل كه تركان خوان يغمارا

Faghān ḳīn lūliyān-i shōkh-i shīrīngār-i shaḥr-āshūb
Chunān burdand ṣabr aż dil ḳeḥ ṭurḳān kh'ān-i yaghmārā.

ز عشق ناتمام ما جمال يار مستغنيست
باب و رنگ و خال و خطّ چه حاجت روي زيبارا

Ża ɛishḳ-i nāṭamām-i mā jamāl-i yār-i musṭaghnīṣṭ
Ba āb wa rang wa khāl wa khaṭṭ cheḥ ḥājaṭ rōyi żēbārā.

حديث از مطرب و مي گو و راز دهر كمتر جو
كه كس نكشود و نكشايد بحكمت اين معمّارا

Ḥadīṣ aż muṭrib wa may gō wa rāż-i daḥar ḳamṭar jō
Keḥ ḳaṣ naḳ'shūd wa naḳ'shāyad baḥiḳmaṭ īn muɛamınārā.

من از آن حسن روز افزون كه يوسف داشت دانستم
كه عشق از پردهٔ عصمت برون آرد زليخارا

Man aż ān ḥuṣn-i rōż-afżūn ḳeh̤ Yūṣuf dāshṭ dāniṣṭam
Ḳeh̤ ɛishḳ aż pardah̤-i ɛiṣmaṭ berūn ārad żulīkhārā,

نصیحت گوش کن جانا که از جان دوستتر دارند
جوانان سعادتمند پند پیر دانارا

Naṣīḥaṭ gōshi ḳun jānā ḳeh̤ aż jān dōṣṭiṭar dārand
Jawānān-i saɛādaṭmand-i pand-i pīr-i dānārā.

بدم گفتي و خرسندم عفاك الله نكو گفتي
جواب تلخ میزیبد لب لعل شکرخوارا

Badam gufṭī wa khurṣandam ɛafāḳ allah̤ neḳō gufṭī
Jawāb-i ṭalkh-i mīżēbad lab-i laɛl-i shaḳarkh'ārā

غزل گفتي و دُر سفتي بيا و خوش بخوان حافظ
که بر نظم تو افشاند فلک عقد ثریارا

Ghażal gufṭī wa durr sufṭī biyā wa khūsh bakh'ān ḥāfiż
Keh̤ bar nāżm-i ṭō afshānad falaḳ ɛiḳdi ṣuriyārā.

In this specimen of Persian writing the learner will observe a few combinations of letters, which he must by no means forget; as لا lāmālif, compounded of ل *l* and ا *a*, in the word مصلا muṣallā: but the most difficult combinations are formed with ج چ ح خ which have the singular property of causing all the preceding letters to rise above the line, as بخارا bokhārā, نخچیر nakhchīr, تصحیح taṣḥīḥ. The letters that precede م *m* are also sometimes raised. (*Note.* It would greatly facilitate the art of printing with Arabic types, if we were to introduce a method of joining all the letters on the same line: and which might be done without occasioning the least inconvenience to the reader. According to this idea we might print the three words, here given as an example, in this manner بخارا نخچیر تصحیح. It appears to have been the ancient practice of the Arabs themselves).

The Arabic characters, like those of the Europeans, are written in a variety of different hands; but the most common of them are the نسخی Niṣkhī, the تعلیق Taɛlīḳ, or *hanging*, and the شکسته Shakaṣṭaḥ, or *broken*. Our books are printed in the Niskhi hand, and all Arabic manuscripts, as well as many Persian and Turkish histories, are written in it; but the Persians write their poetical works in the Taɛlik, which answers to the most elegant of our Italic hands. As to the Shakastah, it is very irregular and inelegant, and is chiefly used as the cursive hand for business and correspondence; but this hand, however difficult and barbarous, must be learned by all men of business in India, as the letters from the princes of the country are seldom written in any other manner. A specimen of these different forms of writing is engraved, and inserted at the end of this Grammar.

OF NOUNS,

AND FIRST OF GENDERS.

The reader will soon perceive with pleasure a great resemblance between the Persian and English languages, in the facility and simplicity of their form and construction; the former, as well as the latter, has no difference of termination to mark the gender, either in substantives or adjectives: all inanimate things are neuter, and animals of different sexes either have different names, as پسر pis̤ar, *a son, a boy*, کنیز kanīz̤, *a girl*, or are distinguished by the words نر nar, *male*, and ماده mādah, *female*; as شیرِ نر shēri nar, *a lion*, شیر ماده shēri mādah, *a lioness*.

Sometimes, indeed, a word is made feminine, after the manner of the Arabians, by having ة added to it, as معشوق maեshūḳ, *a friend*, amicus, معشوقه maեshūḳaẖ *a mistress*, amica, as in this verse:

گل دربر و مي بركف و معشوقه بكامست

Flowers are in my bosom, wine in my hand; and my mistress yields to my desire.

But in general, when the Persians adopt an Arabic noun of the feminine gender, they make it neuter, and change the final ة into ت; thus نعمة naեmaṭ, *a benefit*, is written نعمت: and almost all the Persian nouns ending in ت, which are very numerous, are borrowed from the Arabs.

OF CASES.

The Persian substantives, like ours, have but one variation of case, which is formed by addding the syllable را to the nominative in both numbers; and answers often to the dative, but generally to the accusative case in other languages; as,

Nominative, پسر pisar, *a child.*

Dative and Acc. پسررا pisarrā, *to a child* or *the child.*

When the accusative is used indefinitely, the syllable را is omitted, as گل چیدن gul chīdan, *to gather a flower*, that is, *any flower;* but when the noun is definite or limited, that syllable is added to it, as گلرا چید gulrā chīd, *he gathered the flower*, that is, *the particular flower*. There is no genitive case in Persian, but when two substantives of different meanings come together, a kasra or short *i* (ِ) is added in reading to the former of them, and the latter remains unaltered, as مشک ختن *the musk of Tartary*, which must be read mushki Khotan. The same rule must be observed before a pronoun possessive; as پسر من pisari man, *my child*; and before an adjective; as شمشیرِ تابناک shamshīri ṭābnāg, *a bright scymitar*. If the first word ends in ا or و the letter ي is affixed to it as پاشا pāshā, *a basha*, پاشاي موصل pāshā-i Mūṣal, *the Basha of Mousel*, میوها mīwahā *fruits:* میوهاي شیرین mīwahā-i shīrīn, *sweet fruits:* if nouns ending in ه come before other nouns or adjectives, the mark Hamza ء is added to them, as چشمهٔ حیوان chashmahi ḥaywān, *the fountain of life*.

The other cases are expressed for the most part, as in

our language, by particles placed before the nominative, as,

Vocative, اي پسر ay pisar, *O child.*
Ablative, از پسر aẑ pisar, *from a child.*

The poets, indeed, often form a vocative case by adding to the nominative, as ساقيا sākiyā, *O cup-bearer,* شاها shāhā, *O king;* thus Sadi uses بلبلا bulbulā as the vocative of بلبل bulbul, *a nightingale.*

بلبلا مژده. بهار بيار خبرِ بد ببوم بازبگذار

Bring, O nightingale, the tidings of spring; leave all unpleasant news to the owl.

In some old compositions the particle مر mar is prefixed to the accusative case; as مر اورا ديدم mar ōrā dīdam, *I saw him;* but this is either obsolete or inelegant, and is seldom used by the moderns.

The reader, who has been used to the inflexions of European languages, will, perhaps, be pleased to see an cxample of Persian nouns, as they answer to the cases in Latin:

گل gul, *a rose*, rosa.

	Singular.		Plural.	
Nom.	گل *a rose,*	rosa.	گلها *roses,*	rosæ.
Gen.	گل *of a rose,*	rosæ.	گلها *of roses,*	rosarum.
Dat.	گلرا *to a rose,*	rosæ.	گلهارا *to roses,*	rosis.
Acc.	گلرا *the rose,*	rosam.	گلهارا *the roses,*	rosas.
Voc. اي گل / Poet. گلا	*O rose,*	ô rosa.	اي گلها *O roses,*	ô rosæ.
Abl.	از گل *from a rose,*	rosâ.	از گلها *from roses,*	rosis.

بلبل bulbul, *a nightingale.*

Singular.

Nom. and Gen.	بلبل *a nightingale.*
Dat. and Acc.	بلبلرا *to a nightingale.*
Voc. اي بلبل (Poet. بلبلا)	*O nightingale.*
Abl.	از بلبل *from a nightingale.*

Plural.

Nom. and Gen.	بلبلان *nightingales.*
Dat. and Acc.	بلبلانرا *to nightingales.*
Voc.	اي بلبلان *O nightingales.*
Abl.	از بلبلان *from nightingales*

ساقي بيار باده كه آمد زمان گل
تا بشكنيم توبه دگر در ميان گل
حافظ وصالِ گل طلبي همچو بلبلان
جان كن فداي خاكِ رهِ باغبانِ گل

Boy, bring the wine, for the season of the rose approaches; let us again break our vows of repentance in the midst of the roses. O Hafiz, thou desirest, like the nightingales, the presence of the rose: let thy very soul be a ransom for the earth where the keeper of the rose garden walks!

I shall in this manner quote a few Persian couplets, as examples of the principal rules in this grammar; such quotations will give some variety to a subject naturally barren and unpleasant; will serve as a specimen of the Oriental style; and will be more easily retained in the memory than rules delivered in mere prose.

OF THE ARTICLE.

Our article *a* is supplied in Persian by adding the letter ي to a noun, which restrains it to the singular number; as گلي gulī, *a single rose;*

رفتم بباغ صبحدمي تا چينم گلي
آمد بگوش ناگهم آواز بلبلي

One morning I went into the garden to gather *a* rose, when on a sudden the voice of *a* nightingale struck my ear.

Without this termination گل gul would signify *roses* or *flowers* collectively, as

مي خواه و گل فشان كن

Call for wine, and scatter flowers around.

When a noun ends in ة the idea of unity is expressed by the mark Hamza, as چشمهٔ chashmahi, *a single fountain.*

OF NUMBERS.

From the two examples in a preceding section it appears that the Persian plural is formed by adding ان or ها to the singular: but these terminations are not, as in many languages, wholly arbitrary: on the contrary, they are regulated with the utmost precision. The names of animals form their plural in ان, as

گرگ gurg, *a wolf.* گرگان gurgān, *wolves.*
پلنگ palang, *a tiger.* پلنگان palangān, *tygers.*

but words which signify things without life make their plurals by the addition of the syllable ها, as

بال bāl, *a wing.* بالها bālhā, *wings.*
ساحل sāḥil, *a shore.* ساحلها sāḥilhā, *shores.*

Both these plurals occur in the following elegant distich:

شب تاریک وبیم موج وگردابی چنین هایل
کجا دانند حال ما سبکباران ساحلها

The night is dark; the fear of the waves oppress us, and the whirlpool is dreadful! How should those, who bear light burdens on the shores, know the misery of our situation?

There are, however, a few exceptions to these rules: the names of animals sometimes make their plurals in ها as well as in ان, as شتر shutur, *a camel,* شترها shuturhā and شتران shuturān, *camels;* and on the other side the names of things sometimes have plurals in ان, as لب lab, *a lip,* لبان labān, *lips.*

Names of persons ending in ا or و form their plurals in یان, as دانا dānā, *a learned man*, دانایان dānāyān, *learned men;* and those that end in ه are made plural by changing the last letter into گان, as بچه bachaḥ, *an infant*, بچگان bachagān, *infants;* and sometimes by adding گان as a separate syllable; thus, فرشته farishtaḥ, *an angel*, فرشته گان, farishtaḥ gān, *angels*.

If the name of a thing ends in ه, the final letter is absorbed in the plural before the syllable ها, as خانه khānaḥ *a house*, خانها khānaḥā, *houses*.

In some modern Persian books, as the life of Nader Shah and others, the plural often ends in ات or in جات if the singular has a final ه.

Sing.		Plur.	
نوازش nawāzish,	*a favour.*	نوازشات nawāzishāt,	*favours.*
قلعة kalɛat,	*a castle.*	قلعجات kalɛajāt,	*castles.*

But these must be considered as barbarous, and are a proof that the late dreadful commotions which have ruined the empire of the Persians, have begun to destroy even the beautiful simplicity of their language.

It must not be omitted, that the Arabic substantives frequently have two sorts of plurals, one formed according to the analogy of the Persian nouns, and another after the irregular manner of the Arabians; as عيب ɛayb, *a vice*, عيبها ɛaybhā and عوايب ɛawāyib, *vices*; قلعه kalɛah, *a castle*, قلعها kalɛahā and قلاع kilāɛ, *castles*; نايب nāyib, *a viceroy*, plur. نُوّاب nūwāb, which our countrymen have mistaken for the singular number, and say very improperly *a nabob*.* This is one argument out of a great number to prove the impossibility of learning the Persian language accurately without a moderate knowledge of the Arabic; and if the learner will follow my advice, he will peruse with attention the Arabic grammar of Erpenius† before he attempts to translate a Persian manuscript.

OF ADJECTIVES.

The Persian adjectives admit of no variation, but in the degrees of comparison. The positive is made com-

* It is no mistake. The plural is used in India as a respectful distinction.

† There are two fine editions of this grammar, the first published by the very learned Golius, and the second by the late Albert Schultens; both these Orientalists have added a number of Arabic odes and elegies, which they have explained in excellent notes: but these editions are scarce; and Meninski has inserted in his grammar the substance of Erpenius, with many new remarks.

parative by adding to it تر, and superlative by adding ترين, as

خوب khūb, *fair*, خوبتر khūbtar, *fairer*, خوبترين khūbtarīn, *fairest*.

Our *than* after a comparative is expressed by the preposition از aż, as

بياض روي تو روشنتر از رخِ روز
سواد زلف تو تاريكتر از ظلمتِ داج

The brightness of thy face is more splendid than the cheek of day: the blackness of thy locks is darker than the hue of night.

ماه نيكوست و لي روي تو زيباتر از وست
سروِ دلجوست ولي قدِّ تو دلجوتر از وست

The moon is bright, but thy face is brighter than it; the cypress is graceful, but thy s͡hape is more graceful than the cypress.

An adjective is sometimes used substantively, and forms its plural like a noun, حكيمان ḥaḳīman, *the wise*; if it be a compounded adjective the syllables ان and را, denoting the plural number and the oblique case, are placed at the end of it, as پري رو parī-rō, *angel face;* oblique پري رورا parīrōrā; plural پري رويان parīrōyān; oblique پري رويانرا parīrōyānrā; as

فرو مانند پري رويان زآن عارض
خجل گشتند سمن بويان زآن کاکل

The damsels with faces like angels are dejected at the sight of that cheek; the nymphs with the fragrance of jessamine are filled with envy when they view those curls.

OF PRONOUNS.

The personal pronouns are these which follow;

من man, *I.*

Sing. من man, *I.*		Oblique,	مرا marā, *me.*
Plur. ما mā, *we.*			مارا mārā, *us.*
(or مايان māyān).			(or مايانرا māyānrā).

تو tō, *thou.*

Sing. تو tō,	*thou.*	Obl.	ترا torā,	*thee.*
Plur. شما shumā, *you* or *ye*,*			شمارا shumārā, *you.*	
(or شمايان shumāyān).			(or شمايانرا shumāyānrā).	

* شما shumā is used, as *you* in English, in the singular number, for تو.

او ō, *he.*

Sing. او ō, *he*, *she*, or *it*. Obl. اورا ōrā, *him*, *her*, or *it*.
Plur. ايشان ēshān, *they*. ايشانرا ēshānrā, *them*.

The poets often use شان for ايشان, as

همیرفتم وکوفتم مغز شان
تهي کردم از پیکر نغز شان

I went, and bruised their helmets; I disfigured their beautiful faces.

After a preposition او is often changed into وي or و or اوي, as

چون شاه جهاندار بنمود روي
زمینرا ببوسید و شد پیش اوي

When the king of the world showed his face, the general kissed the ground, and advanced before him. *Ferdusi.*

Sometimes after the preposition ب *in*, the letter د is inserted to prevent the hiatus, as بدو badō for باو ba-ō, *to him;* the same may be observed of بدان badān for بان ba-ān, *to that*, بدين badīn for باين *to this.**

* In the same manner, and from the same motives, the old Romans added a *d* to many words followed by a vowel; thus Horace, if we adopt the reading of Muretus, uses *tibid* for *tibi*,

Omne crede diem *tibid* illuxisse supremum.

The possessives are the same with the personals, and are distinguished by being added to their substantives; as

Sing. دلِ من dili man, *my heart.*

دلِ تو dili tō, *thy heart.*

دلِ او dili ō, or دلِ وي dili way, *his* or *her heart.*

Plur. دلهاي ما dilhāï mā, *our hearts.*

دلهاي شما dilhāï shumā *your hearts.*

Poet. تان

دلهاي ايشان dilhāï ēshān, *their hearts.*

Poet. شان

They are often expressed in the singular number by these final letters (with the short ă pronounced before them), م am, ت at, and ش ash, and after an ا or ه by ام am, ات at, and اش ash: but after nouns ending in ا alif or و wāw the letter ي yā is inserted before the finals م ت ش; as

دلم dilam, *my heart.*

دلت dilat, *thy heart.*

دلش dilash, *his* or *her heart.*

جامهٔ ام jāmahi am, *my robe.*

جامهٔ ات jāmahi at *thy robe.*

جامهٔ اش jāmahi ash, *his* or *her robe.*

مویم mōyam, *my hair.*
مویت mōyat, *thy hair.*
مویش mōyash, *his* or *her hair.*

In poetry, and sometimes in prose, the oblique cases of the personal pronouns are also expressed by ش ت م, as

خوشا شیراز و وضع بی مثالش
خداوندا نگه‌دار از زوالش

Joy be to Shiraz and its charming borders! O heaven, preserve *it* from decay!

These oblique cases are joined to any word in the sentence which the poet finds convenient; thus in the couplet just quoted the pronoun ش *it*, is added to زوال; so in the following distich, ت the dative of تو *thou*, is placed after the conjunction گر gar, *if*.

بمی سجاده رنگین کن گرت پیر مغان گوید
که سالک بیخبر نبود زراه و رسم منزلها

Tinge the sacred carpet with wine, if the master of the feast orders *thee*; for he that travels is not ignorant of the ways and manners of banquet-houses.

Our reciprocal pronouns *own* and *self* are expressed in

Persian by the following words, which are applicable to all persons and sexes; as

Nom.	خود or خودش	Oblique,	خودرا
	خويشتن or خويش		خويشتن را
	or خوي		

thus we may use

من خود *myself.*	ما خود *ourselves.*
تو خود *thyself.*	شما خود *yourselves.*
او خود *his* or *herself.*	ايشان خود *theirselves.**

خود is also joined like the Latin *ipse* to every person of a verb, as

Sing.	Plur.
خود آمدم *ipse veni.*	خود آمديم *ipsi venimus.*
خود آمدي *ipse venisti.*	خود آمديد *ipsi venistis.*
خود آمد *ipse venit.*	خود آمدند *ipsi venerunt.*

* I here use *his self* and *their selves* instead of the corrupted words *himself* and *themselves;* in which usage I am justified by the authority of Sidney, and of other writers in the reign of Elizabeth: *self* seems to have been originally a noun, and was perhaps a synonymous word for *soul*, according to Locke's definition of it: " *Self* is " that conscious thinking thing, which is sensible or conscious of pleasure and pain, " capable of happiness and misery." If this observation be just, the Arabs have exactly the same idiom, for their نفس *soul*, answers precisely to our *self*, as صبي رمي نفسه في نهر " a boy threw *his self* into a river."

The word خود seems to be redundant in the following beautiful lines of Sadi,

داني چه گفت مرا آن بلبل سحري
تو خود چه آدمي كز عشق بي‌خبري

Dost thou know what the early nightingale said to me?
"What sort of man art thou, that canst be ignorant of
"love?"

When خود is used as a pronoun possessive, it answers to the Greek σφέτερος, and signifies *my*, *thy*, *our*, *your*, *his* or *her*, and *their*, according to the person and number of the principal verb in the sentence: as in this couplet of Hafiz,

محرم راز دل شيداي خود
كس نمي بينم زخاصّ و عام را

I see no man, either among the nobles or the populace, to
whom I can trust the secret of *my* afflicted heart.

The demonstrative pronouns are the following:

اين in, *this.*

Sing.	اين *this.*	Oblique cases,	اينرا
Plur.	اينان *these.*		اينانرا
or	اينها		or اينهارا

آن ān, *that.*

Sing. آن *that.* Oblique cases, آنرا

Plur. آنان *those.* انانرا

or آنها or آنهارا

When این īn is prefixed to a noun, so as to form one word, it is frequently changed into اِم im, as امشب imshab, *to night;*

تعالي الله چه دولت دارم امشب
که آمد ناگهان دلدارم امشب

Heaven! how great is my happiness this night! for this night is my beloved come unexpectedly!

and امروز imrōz, *to-day;*

روز عیش و طرب و عید صیامست امروز
کام دل حاصل و ایام بکامست امروز

This day is a day of mirth, and joy, and the feast of spring; this day my heart obtains its desires, and fortune is favourable.

The words آن and از آن prefixed to pronouns *personal*, change them into *possessives*, and are read with a short vowel, آنِ تو ānī tō, or از آنِ تو až āni tō, i. e. *thine*, as

ماه کنعان من مسند مصر آنِ تو شد

O my moon of Canaan (O Joseph), the throne of Egypt is *thine!*

The relatives and interrogatives are supplied by the invariable pronouns كه keh and چه cheh, of which the former usually relates to persons, and the latter to things, in the oblique cases of these pronouns the final ه is absorbed before the syllable را, as

Nom. كه *who.* Oblique, كرا *whom.*

چه *which.* چرا *which.*

كي kī and چي chī are interrogatives, and are very often joined to the verb است, as كيست *who is it?* چيست *what is it?*

يا رب ان شاهوش ماه رخ زهره جبين
دُرّ يكتاي كه و گوهر يكدانه كيست

O heaven! whose precious pearl, and whose inestimable jewel is that royal maid, with a cheek like the moon, and a forehead like Venus;

كدام kadām (properly *which?*) is also an interrogative pronoun, as

ميخواره و سرگشته و رنديم و نظرباز
وآنكس كه چنين نيست در اين شهر كدامست

We are fond of wine, wanton, dissolute, and with rolling eyes; but *who* is there in this city that has not the same vices?

Our *soever* is expressed in Persian by هر ẖar or هران ẖarān prefixed to the relatives, as

هرکه and هرانکه *whosoever.* each

هرچه and هرانچه *whatsoever.*

OF VERBS.

The Persians have active and neuter verbs like other nations; but many of their verbs have both an active and neuter sense, which can be determined only by the construction. These verbs have properly but one conjugation, and but three changes of tense; the imperative, the aorist, and the preterite; all the other tenses being formed by the help of the particles مي mī and همي ẖamī, or of the auxiliary verbs هستن ẖaṣṭan or بودن būdan, *to be*, and خواستن kh'āṣṭan, *to want, will* or *be willing*. The passive voice is formed by adding the tenses of the verb substantive شدن shudan to the participle preterite of the active; خوانده شد kh'āndaẖ shud, *it was read.* The inflexions of these auxiliaries must be here exhibited, and must be learned by heart, as they will be very useful in forming the compound tenses of the active verbs.

بودن būdan, *to be.*

The present tense of this verb is irregular, but very easy, and must be carefully remembered, as it is the model for the variations of persons in all tenses.

Indicative Mood, Present Tense.

Sing.	Plur.
ام am, *I am.*	ايم ēm, *we are.*
اي ī *thou art.*	ايد ēd, *ye are.*
است ast, *he is.*	اند and, *they are.*

This tense joined to nouns, pronouns, or adjectives, often coalesces with them, and loses the initial short ا alif; as with pronouns,

Sing.	Plur.
منم manam, *ego sum.*	مايم mā ēm, *nos sumus.*
تويي tō yī, *tu es.*	شمايد shamā-ēd, *vos estis.*
اوست ō-ast *ille est.*	ايشانند ēshān and, *illi sunt.*

With adjectives,

Sing.	Plur.
شادم shād am, *I am glad.*	شاديم shādēm, *we are glad.*
شادي shād ī, *thou art glad.*	شاديد shād ēd, *you are glad.*
شادست shād ast, *he is glad.*	شادند shād and, *they are glad.*

The negatives are formed by prefixing نه naḥ or ن na, as نه ام *I am not*, &c. but نه است is commonly written نيست nēṣṭ, *there is not*, as

راهيست راه عشق كه هيچش كناره نيست
آنجا جز آنكه جان بسپارند چاره نيست

The path of love is a path to which there is no end, in which there is no remedy for lovers, but to give up their souls. *Hafiz.*

Second Present from the defective هستن haṣṭan, *to be.*

Sing.	Plur.
هستم *I am.*	هستيم *we are.*
هستي *thou art.*	هستيد *you are.*
هست *he is.*	هستند *they are.*

Preterite.

Sing.	Plur.
بودم *I was.*	بوديم *we were.*
بودي *thou wast.*	بوديد *you were.*
بود *he was.*	بودند *they were.*

Preterite Imperfect.

مي بودم مي بودي مي بود &c.

Compound Preterite.

Sing.	Plur.
بوده ام *I have been.*	بوده ايم *we have been.*
بوده اي or بودهٔ *thou hast been.*	بوده ايد *you have been.*
بوده است *he has been.*	بوده اند *they have been.*

Preterpluperfect.

بوده شدم *I had been.*	بوده شديم *we had been.*
بوده شدي *thou hadst been.*	بوده شديد *you had been.*
بوده شد *he had been.*	بوده شدند *they had been.*

Future.

خواهم بود *I will be.*	خواهيم بود *we will be.*
خواهي بود *thou wilt be.*	خواهيد بود *you will be.*
خواهد بود *he will be.*	خواهند بود *they will be.*

Imperative.

	باشيم *let us be.*
باش or بو *be thou.*	باشيد *be ye.*
باشد or باد *let him be*	باشند *let them be.*

Subjunctive, or Aorist,

Sing.	Plur.
باشم or بوم *I be.*	باشيم or بويم *we be.*
باشي or بوي *thou beest.*	باشيد or بويد *you be.*
باشد or بود *he be.*	باشند or بوند *they be.*

Potential.

بودمي *I would be.*	بوديمي *we would be.*
بودي *thou wouldst be*	بوديدي *you would be.*
بودي *he would be.*	بودندي *they would be.*

Future Subjunctive.

بوده باشم *I shall have been.*	بوده باشيم *we shall have been.*
بوده باشي *thou shalt have been.*	بوده باشيد *you shall have been.*
بوده باشد *he shall have been.*	بوده باشند *they shall have been.*

Infinitive.

Present, بودن by contraction بود *to be.*

Preterite, بوده شدن *to have been.*

Participles.

باشا *being.* بوده *been.*

شدن shudan, *to be,*

used in forming the Passive voice.

Indicative Present.

Sing.	Plur.
مي شوم *I am.*	مى شويم *we are.*
مي شوي *thou art.*	مي شويد *you are.*
مي شود *he is.*	مي شوند *they are.*

Preterite.

شدم *I was.*	شديم *we were.*
شدي *thou wast.*	شديد *you were.*
شد *he was.*	شدند *they were.*

Preterite Imperfect.

مي شدم مي شدي مي شد &c.

Compound Preterite.

شده ام *I have been.*	شده ايم *we have been.*
شده اي or شدهٔ *thou hast been.*	شده ايد *you have been*
شده است *he has been.*	شده اند *they have been.*

Preterpluperfect.

شده بودم *I had been.*	شده بوديم *we had been.*
شده بودي *thou hadst been.*	شده بوديد *you had been.*
شده بود *he had been*	شده بودند *they had been.*

Future.

Sing.	Plur.
خواهم شد *I will be.*	خواهيم شد *we will be.*
خواهي شد *thou wilt be.*	خواهيد شد *you will be.*
خواهد شد *he will be.*	خواهند شد *they will be.*

Imperative.

———	شويم *let us be.*
شو *be thou.*	شويد *be ye.*
شود *let him be.*	شوند *let them be.*

Subjunctive, or Aorist.

شوم *I be.*	شويم *we be.*
شوي *thou beest.*	شويد *you be.*
شود *he be.*	شوند *they be.*

Infinitive.

شدن *to be.* شده بودن *to have been.*

Participles.

شوا *being.* شده *having been.*

خواستن kh'āṣṭan or خواهيدن kh'āḥīdan, *to be willing.*

Aorist,

used in forming the Compound Future of verbs.

Sing.	Plur.
خواهم *I will.*	خواهيم *we will.*
خواهي *thou wilt.*	خواهيد *you will.*
خواهد *he will.*	خواهند *they will.*

The other tenses are formed like those of the regular verbs.

OF TENSES.

It will here be useful to exhibit an analysis of all the tenses of a Persian verb, and to shew in what manner they are deduced from the infinitive, which is properly considered by the Oriental grammarians as the spring and fountain of all the moods and tenses, and which, therefore, is called in Arabic مصدر maṣdar, or *the source.*

All regular infinitives end in يدن, as رسيدن raṣīdan, *to arrive*, ناليدن nālīdan, *to grieve*, ترسيدن, ṭarṣīdan, *to fear.*

The third person of the preterite is formed by rejecting ن from the infinitive, رسيد *he arrived,* ناليد *he grieved,* ترسيد *he feared.*

گفتم مگر صبا زچمن رسید
یا کاروان مشك زراه ختن رسید

I said, is the zephyr breathing from the garden? or is a caravan of musk coming from Khoten?

The letter ب prefixed to this tense is often redundant, as جامه‌را ببرد و برفت *he took the mantle, and departed.*

From the preterite is formed the imperfect tense by prefixing the particles مي or همي, as ميرسيد or همي‌رسيد *he was arriving.*

In the third persons the imperfect tense is sometimes expressed by adding ي to the preterite, as ناليدي *he was grieving,* ناليدندي *they were grieving;* this form is common in prose, as

بطرب و نشاط مشغول بودندي و نغمه ترانه از زبان چنگ
چغانه استماع نمودندي

They were immersed in pleasure and delight, and were constantly listening to the melody of the lute, and of the cymbal.

The same letter ي added to the first and third persons of the past tense, forms the potential mood, as ناليدمي *I might, could, should,* or *would grieve,* نالیدیمی *we might, &c. grieve;* so Ferdusi in a love song,

شبي در برت گر بر آسودمي
سر فخر بر آسمان سودمي

If I could sleep one night on thy bosom, I should seem to touch the sky with my exalted head.

And Hafiz,

آن طرّه که هر جعدش صد نافهء چین ارزد
خوش بودي اگر بودي بویش از خوشخوي

Those locks, each curl of which is worth a hundred musk-bags of China, would be sweet indeed if their scent proceeded from sweetness of temper.

The participle preterite is formed from the infinitive by changing ن into ه, as, رسیده *arrived,* پاشیده *sprinkled,* from which participle and the auxiliary verbs بودن and شدن are made several compound tenses, and the passive voice; as پاشیده ام *I have sprinkled,* پاشیده بودم *I had sprinkled,* پاشیده باشم *I shall have sprinkled,* پاشیده شدم *I was sprinkled.*

هم جان بدان دو نرگس جادو سپرده ایم
هم دل بدان دو سنبل هندو نهاده ایم

We *have* given up all our souls to those two inchanting narcissuses (eyes), we have placed all our hearts on those two black hyacinths (locks of hair).

The Persians are very fond of the participle preterite; and it is very often used by their elegant writers to connect the members of a sentence, and to suspend the sense till the close of a long period: in poetry it sometimes is used like the third person preterite of a verb, as in this fine couplet:

فروغ جام و قدح نور ماه پوشیده
عذار مغبچگان راه آفتاب زده

The brightness of the cup and the goblet obscures the light of the moon; the cheeks of the young cup-bearers steal the splendour of the sun.

In the ode from which this couplet is taken every distich ends with the word زده for زد *he struck.*

In composition the infinitive is contracted by rejecting ن, as خواهم شد *I will be;* so Hafiz,

نفس باد صبا مشک فشان خواهد شد
عالم پیر دگر باره جوان خواهد شد

The breath of the western gale will soon shed musk around; the old world will again be young.

This short infinitive is likewise used after impersonal verbs as توان کرد *it is possible to do;* باید کرد *it is necessary to do;* thus Hafiz, the Anacreon of Persia,

بسعي خود نتوان برد گوهر مقصود
خیال تست که این کار بیحواله برآید

It is impossible to attain the jewel of thy wishes by thy own endeavours; it is a vain imagination to think that it will come to thee without assistance.

And the poet quoted in the history of Cazvini,

روزگار نامه کردار شماست
برآنجا کردار نیکو باید گماشت

The life of man is a journal, in which he must write only good actions.

The imperative is regularly formed by throwing away the termination یدن from the infinitive, as رس *arrive thou,* from رسیدن *to arrive;* the letter ب is often prefixed to the imperative, as بگو *say thou;* بترس *fear thou;* so Ferdusi in his noble satire against a king who had slighted him:

ايا شاه محمود كشوركشاي
زمن گر نترسي بترس از خداي
خيزيدي چرا خاطر تيز من
نترسيدي از تيغ خون ريز من

O king Mahmud, thou conqueror of regions, if thou fearest not me, at least *fear* God! why hast thou inflamed my wrathful temper? dost thou not dread my blood-dropping sword?

It must here be observed, that the negatives نه nah and ن na are changed in the imperative into مه mah and م ma, as مپرس *do not ask;*

درد عشقي كشيده‌ام كه مپرس
زهر هجري چشيده‌ام كه مپرس

I have felt the pain of love; *ask not* of whom; I have tasted the poison of absence; *ask not* from whom.

Before verbs beginning with ا alif the letters ن م and ب are changed into ني, مي and بي, as before آر are used بيار *bring thou,* ميار *do not bring;*

ساقيا ساغر شراب بيهر
يكدو ساغر شراب نهب بيار

Boy, *bring* a cup of wine; *bring* a few more cups of pure wine.

گو شمع میارید در این جمع که امشب
در مجلس ما ماه رخ دوست تمامست
در مجلس ما عطر میامیز که جانرا
هر دم زسر زلف تو خوش بوي مشامست

Say, *bring no* tapers into our assembly, for this night the moon of my beloved's cheek is at its full in our banquet; *sprinkle no* perfume in our apartment, for to our minds the fragrance that constantly proceeds from thy locks is sufficiently pleasing.

The contracted participle used in compound epithets is exactly the same with the imperative, as انگیز *excite thou* عشرت انگیز *mirth-exciting*, افروز *inflame thou*, گیتي افروز *world-inflaming*, Gēti-afrōz, the name of a fairy in the Persian tales translated by Colonel Dow.

The participles of the present tense are formed by adding ا ان, or نده to the imperative, as رسان, رسا and رسنده *arriving*; which last participle is often used for a noun of action, as بازنده *a player*.

From the imperative also is formed the conjunctive tense or aorist by adding to it the usual personal termination, as from آي *come thou*, آيم *I may* or *will come*.

چو آفتاب مي از مشرق پياله برآيد
زباغ عارض ساقي هزار لاله برآيد

When the sun of the wine shall rise from the east of the cup, a thousand tulips will spring from the garden of the cup-bearer's cheek.

By this affected, yet lively allegory, the poet only means that "the cup-bearer will blush when he shall present the "wine to the guests."

For the most part this form of the Persian verb, which the grammarians properly call the aorist, or indefinite tense, answers to the potential mood of other languages, and is governed by conjunctions as in Latin and English: this will be seen more clearly in the following example taken from the life of Nader Shah;

دانايان رموز آگاهي و دقيقه يابان حكمتهاي آلهي واضح است
كه در هر عهد و اوان كه اوضاع جهان مختلف و پريشان و بر
چرخ ستمگر بكام ستمكيشان گردد خداوند يكانه كه مدبر

این کارخانه و مقلّب اوضاع زمانه است از فیض بی منتهاي خود سعادتمندیرا مویّد و درعرصهٔ گیتي مبسوط الید کند که بمراهم مراحم و رافت بالتیام جراحات قلوب ستمدیدگان پردازد و مذاق تمناي تلخکامان زهر حوادث را بشهد عدالت شیرین سازد

It is evident to the discerning and intelligent part of mankind, that, whenever the affairs of the world are thrown into confusion, and fortune favours the desires of the unjust, the great Disposer of events, in the effusion of his endless mercy, selects some fortunate hero, whom he supports with his eternal favour; and whom he commands to heal with the balm of benevolence the wounds of the afflicted, and to sweeten the bitter draught of their misfortunes with the honey of justice.

In which period the words گردد gardad, کند kunad, پردازد pardāżad, and سازد ṣāżad, are the aorists of گردیدن gardīdan, کردن kardan, پرداختن pardākhṭan, and ساختن ṣākhṭan, governed by the conjunction که *that.*

The present tense is formed by prefixing مي or همي to the aorist, as ميدانم *I know*, ميداني *thou knowest*, ميداند *he knoweth*:

اي باد صبا بگذر آنجا كه تو ميدايي
واحوال دلم به‌گو پيدا كه تو ميداني

O gentle gale, pass by the place which *thou knowest*, and disclose the secrets of my heart which *thou knowest*.

زين خوش رقم كه بر گل رخسار ميكشي
خطّ بر صحيفه گل كلزار ميكشي

With that sweet hue which *thou bearest* on the rose of thy cheek, *thou drawest* a line over the face of the garden-rose.

The particles مي and همي are sometimes joined to the verb, and sometimes separated from it, according to the pleasure of the writer, as

بعيش كوش كه تا چشم ميزني برهم
خزان هميرسد و نوبهار مي گذرد

Pursue thy pleasures eagerly, for while thou canst close thine eye, the autumn is *approaching*, and the fresh season is *passing* away.

The letter ب prefixed to the aorist restrains it to the future tense, as برسم *I will arrive;* thus Nakshebi in his work called طوطي نامه or *the Tales of a Parrot*, Night 35,

نخشبي جد و جهد بايد كرد
چونكه مردم بيار خود برسد
هر كه در كارها كند جهدي
عاقبت بر مراد خود برسد

O Nakshebi, a man who desires to enjoy his beloved must be active and diligent: whoever labours diligently in his affairs, *will* at last *attain* the object of his wishes.

After having given this analysis of the Persian verb, it will be necessary to add a table of the moods and tenses as they answer to those of European languages.

Verb Active, پرسيدن pursīdan, *to ask.*

Indicative Mood, Present Tense.

Sing.	Plur.
مي پرسم *I ask.*	مي پرسيم *we ask.*
مي پرسي *thou askest.*	مي پرسيد *you ask.*
مي پرسد *he asks.*	مي پرسند *they ask.*

Simple Preterite.

Sing.	Plur.
پرسيدم *I asked.*	پرسيديم *we asked.*
پرسيدي *thou askedst.*	پرسيديد *you asked.*
پرسيد *he asked.*	پرسيدند *they asked.*

Compound Preterite.

پرسيده ام *I have asked.*	پرسيده ايم *we have asked.*
پرسيده اي or پرسيدهء *thou hast asked.*	پرسيده ايد *you have asked.*
پرسيده است or پرسيداست *he has asked.*	پرسيده اند *they have asked.*

Preterite Imperfect.

مي پرسيدم *I was asking.*	مي پرسيديم *we were asking.*
مي پرسيدي *thou wast asking.*	مي پرسيديد *you were asking.*
مي پرسيد *he was asking.*	مي پرسيدند *they were asking.*

Preterpluperfect.

پرسيده بودم *I had asked.*	پرسيده بوديم *we had asked.*
پرسيده بودي *thou hadst asked.*	پرسيده بوديد *you had asked.*
پرسيده بود *he had asked.*	پرسيده بودند *they had asked.*

First Future.

Sing.	Plur.
بپرسم *I shall ask.*	بپرسيم *we shall ask.*
بپرسي *thou shalt ask.*	بپرسيد *you shall ask.*
بپرسد *he shall ask.*	بپرسند *they shall ask.**

Second Future.

خواهم پرسيد *I will ask.*	خواهيم پرسيد *we will ask.*
خواهي پرسيد *thou wilt ask.*	خواهيد پرسيد *you will ask.*
خواهد پرسيد *he will ask.*	خواهند پرسيد *they will ask.*

Imperative.

———	پرسيم *let us ask.*
پرس or بپرس *ask thou.*	پرسيد *ask you.*
پرسد *let him ask.*	پرسند *let them ask.*

Conjunctive or Aorist.

پرسم *I may ask.*	پرسيم *we may ask.*
پرسي *thou mayst ask.*	پرسيد *you may ask.*
پرسد *he may ask.*	پرسند *they may ask.*

Potential.

پرسيدمي *I might, &c. ask.*	پرسيديمي *we might, &c. ask.*
پرسيدي *thou mighst ask.*	پرسيديدي *you might ask.*
پرسيدي *he might ask.*	پرسيدندي *they might ask.*

* This form is also commonly used for the imperative, as بپرسم *let me ask*, &c.

Compound Future.

Sing. پرسیده باشم *I shall have asked.*

پرسیده باشي *thou shalt have asked.*

پرسیده باشد *he shall have asked.*

Plur. پرسیده باشیم *we shall have asked.*

پرسیده باشید *you shall have asked.*

پرسیده باشند *they shall have asked.*

Infinitive.

Present, پرسیدن *to ask*, contracted پرسید

Preterite, پرسیده بودن *to have asked.*

Participles.

Present, پرسان and پرسنده *asking, who asks.*

Preterite, پرسیده *asked* or *having asked.*

Passive Voice.

Indicative Present.

Sing. پرسیده مي شوم *I am asked.*

پرسیده مي شوي *thou art asked.*

پرسیده مي شود *he is asked.*

Plur. پرسیده مي شویم *we are asked.*

پرسیده مي شوید *you are asked.*

پرسیده مي شوند *they are asked.*

Preterite.

Sing.	پرسیده شدم	*I was asked.*
	پرسیده شدي	*thou wast asked.*
	پرسیده شد	*he was asked.*
Plur.	پرسیده شدیم	*we were asked.*
	پرسیده شدید	*you were asked*
	پرسیده شدند	*they were asked.*

Preterpluperfect.

Sing.	پرسیده شده بودم	*I had been asked.*
	پرسیده شده بودي	*thou hadst been asked*
	پرسیده شده بود	*he had been asked.*
Plur.	پرسیده شده بودیم	*we had been asked.*
	پرسیده شده بودید	*you had been asked.*
	پرسیده شده بودند	*they had been asked.*

Aorist.

Sing.	پرسیده شوم	*I may be asked.*
	پرسیده شوي	*thou mayst be asked.*
	پرسیده شود	*he may be asked.*
Plur.	پرسیده شویم	*we may be asked.*
	پرسیده شوید	*you may be asked.*
	پرسیده شوند	*they may be asked.*

Second Future.

Sing. پرسیده خواهم شد *I shall be asked.*
پرسیده خواهي شد *thou shalt be asked.*
پرسیده خواهد شد *he shall be asked.*
Plur. پرسیده خواهیم شد *we shall be asked.*
پرسیده خواهید شد *you shall be asked.*
پرسیده خواهند شد *they shall be asked.*

Infinitive.

Present, پرسیده شدن *to be asked.*
Preterite, پرسیده شده بودن *to have been asked.*

Negative verbs are formed by prefixing نه or ن to the affirmative in all the tenses, as

Sing.	نمي دانم	*I do not know,*	nescio.
	نمي داني	*thou dost not know,*	nescis.
	نمي داند	*he does not know,*	nescit.
Plur.	نمي دانیم	*we do not know,*	nescimus.
	نمي دانید	*you do not know,*	nescitis.
	نمي دانند	*they do not know,*	nesciunt.

ندانم ازچه سبب رنگ آشناي نیست
سهي قدان سیه چشم ماه سیمارا

I know not why the damsels, tall as cypresses, with black eyes, bright as the moon, have not the colour of love.

Hafiz.

OF IRREGULAR VERBS.

In the ancient language of Persia there were very few or no irregularities: the imperative, which is often irregular in the modern Persian, was anciently formed from the infinitive by rejecting the termination یدن īdan; for originally all infinitives ended in دن dan, till the Arabs introduced their harsh consonants before that syllable, which obliged the Persians, who always affected a sweetness of pronunciation, to change the old termination of some verbs into تن tan, and by degrees the original infinitives grew quite obsolete; yet they still retain the ancient imperatives and the aorists which are formed from them. This little irregularity is the only anomalous part of the Persian language, which, nevertheless, far surpasses in simplicity all other languages, ancient or modern, of which I have any knowledge. This remark on the formation of the Persian imperatives from an obsolete verb, may be useful to those who are curious in ancient dialects; as it will enable them to trace out a considerable part of the old Persian language or Pehlevian پلوي which has the same relation to the modern دري or Persic, as the Icelandic has to the Danish, or the Saxon to the English; and which was, perhaps, spoken in the age of Xenophon. This is the language in which the works of Zeratusht or Zoroaster are preserved, and into which the fables of Bidpai or Pilpai were first translated from the Indian; but as we rejected the Saxon alphabet to admit the Roman; so the Persians, when they embraced the religion of Mahomet, adopted the characters in which the Alcoran was written, and incorporated into their language a multitude of Arabic words and phrases.

The Persian verbs that form their imperatives, and consequently their aorists, from obsolete infinitives, may be distributed into the following classes: the old infinitives may be found by adding يدن īdan to the imperatives, and the aorists by adding to them the personal terminations.

I.

Irregulars that form their imperatives by rejecting تن or د ن

Infin.		Imper.	Aorist.
آختن	*to draw a sabre*	آخ	آخم
اژدن	*to sow together*	اژ	اژم
آزاردن	*to rebuke*	آزار	آزارم
اغوشتن	*to embrace*	اغوش	اغوشم
اغیشتن	*to cut*	اغیش	اغیشم
افشاردن	*to speak idly*	افشار	افشارم
افشاندن	*to sprinkle*	افشان	افشانم
افشردن	*to press*	افشر	افشرم
افگندن or اوگندن	*to throw down*	افگن	افگنم
آگندن	*to fill*	آگن	آگنم
آوُردن	*to bring*	آر and آور	آرم and آورم
بافتن	*to tinge, to weave*	باف	بافم
بُردن	*to bear*	بَر	برم
پروردن	*to feed, cherish*	پرور	پرورم
پژمردن	*to wither*	پژمر	پژمرم
بودن	*to be*	بو	بوم
خواندن	*to read*	خوان	خوانم

Infin.	Imper.	Aorist.
خوردن *to eat*	خور	خورم
راندن *to drive*	ران	رانم
ریستن *to buz*	ریس	ریسم
سپردن *to resign, give in charge*	سپر and سپار	سپرم and سپارم
ستردن *to shave*	ستر	سترم
شاندن *to comb*	شان	شانم
شگافتن *to cleave*	شگاف	شگافم
شکردن *to hunt*	شکر	شکرم
شمردن *to number*	شُمار	شمارم
شنودن *to hear*	شنو	شنوم
غنودن *to slumber*	غنو	غنوم
فسردن *to freeze*	فسر	فسرم
فشردن for افشردن } *to press*	فشر and فشار	فشرم فشارم
فگندن for افگندن } *to throw*	فگن	فگنم
گزاردن *to perform*	گزار	گزارم
گستردن *to strow, spread*	گستر	گسترم
کشتن *to kill*	کش	کشم
کشِفتن *to scatter*	کشوف	کشوفم

Infin.	Imper.	Aorist.
لاندن *to move*	لان	لانم
ماندن *to remain*	مان	مانم
نشاندن *to fix*	نشان	نشانم
هیشتن and هشتن } *to lay down*	هیش	هیشم

II.

Irregulars that change و into اي

آزمودن *to try*	آزماي	آزمايم
اسودن *to rest*	آساي	آسايم
افزودن or فزودن } *to increase*	افزاي or فزاي	افزايم or فزايم
آلودن *to defile*	آلاي	آلايم

The participle of this verb, used in compound adjectives is, آلود, as خواب آلود *sleepy, drowned, in sleep.*

اندودن *to besmear*	انداي	اندايم
پالودن *to strain*	پالاي	پالايم
پيمودن *to measure*	پيماي	پيمايم
زدودن *to polish*	زداي	زدايم
ستودن *to praise*	ستاي	ستايم

Infin.	Imper.	Aorist.
سودن *to stroke*	ساي	سايم
فرمودن *to command*	فرماي	فرمايم
نمودن *to show*	نماي	نمايم
كشودن and كشادن } *to open*	كشاي	كشايم

III,

Irregulars that change ف into ب or و.

آشوفتن آشفتن } *to disturb*	آشوب	آشوبم
تافتن *to inflame*	تاب	تابم
دريافتن *to understand*	درياب	دريابم
سفتن *to bore*	سنب	سنبم

This imperative is very anomalous.

شتافتن *to hasten*	شتاب	شتابم
شگفتن *to blossom*	شگيب	شگيبم
فريفتن *to deceive*	فريب	فريبم
كوفتن *to smite*	كوب	كوبم
نهفتن *to lie hid*	نهبن	

I have never met with this strange imperative.

يافتن *to find*	ياب	يابم
رفتن *to go*	رو	روم

Infin.	Imper.	Aorist.
کافتن *to dig*	کاو	کاوم
گفتن *to say*	گو	گویم
	and گوي	
شنفتن *to hear*	شنو	شنوم

IV.

Irregulars that change خ into ز, س into ش

Infin.	Imper.	Aorist.
افراختن *to exalt*	افراز	افرازم
افروختن *to inflame*	افروز	افروزم
آموختن *to learn*	آموز	آموزم
آمیختن *to mix*	آمیز	آمیزم
انداختن *to throw*	انداز	اندازم
اندوختن *to gain*	اندوز	اندوزم
انگیختن *to excite*	انگیز	انگیزم
آویختن *to hang*	آویز	آویزم
باختن *to play*	باز	بازم
پرداختن *to finish*	پرداز	پردازم
پرهیختن *to beware*	پرهیز	پرهیزم
پختن *to boil*	پز	پزم
بیختن *to sift*	بیز	بیزم
پیختن *to take captive*	پیز	پیزم
تاختن *to twist*	تاز	تازم

Infin.	Imper.	Aorist.
توختن *to collect*	توز	توزم
ریختن *to pour*	ریز	ریزم
ساختن *to prepare, make*	ساز	سازم
سپوختن *to prick*	سپوز	سپوزم
سوختن *to burn*	سوز	سوزم
گداختن *to melt*	گداز	گدازم
گریختن *to flee*	گریز	گریزم
نواختن *to soothe*	نواز	نوازم
شناختن *to understand*	شناس	شناسم
فروختن *to sell*	فروش	فروشم

V.

Irregulars that change ش into ر

انباشتن *to fill*	انبار	انبارم
انکاشتن *to think*	انکار	انکارم
اوباشتن *to swallow*	اوبار	اوبارم
برداشتن *to raise*	بردار	بردارم
پنداشتن *to suppose*	پندار	پندارم
داشتن *to have*	دار	دارم
گذاشتن *to leave*	گذار	گذارم
گذشتن *to pass*	گذر	گذرم
گماشتن *to loose, dismiss*	گمار	گمارم

VI.

Irregulars that reject س

Infin.	Imper.	Aorist.
اجستن *to plant*	اج	اجم
آراستن *to adorn, arrange*	آراي	آرايم
بايستن *to be necessary*	باي	بايم
پايستن *to accept*	پاي	پايم
پيراستن *to deck*	پيراي	پيرايم
جستن *to seek*	جوي	جويم
دانستن *to know*	دان	دانم
رستن *to grow*	روي	رويم
زستن *to live*	زي	زيم
شستن *to wash*	شوي	شويم
گريستن *to weep*	گري	گريم
مانستن *to resemble*	مان	مانم
نگرستن *to view*	نگر	نگرم

VII.

Irregulars in ين

آفريدن *to create*	آفرين	آفرينم
چيدن *to gather*	چين	چينم
ديدن *to see*	بين	بينم
گزيدن *to choose*	گزين	گزينم

VIII.

Irregulars in یر that reject ف

Infin.	Imper.	Aorist.
پذیرفتن *to accept*	پذیر	پذیرم
گرفتن *to take*	گیر	گیرم

IX.

Irregulars that change س into ه

Infin.	Imper.	Aorist.
جستن *to leap*	جه	جهم
رستن *to be delivered*	ره	رهم
خواستن *to be willing, want*	خواه	خواهم
کاستن *to lessen*	کاه	کاهم

X.

Irregulars that change س into ن or ند

Infin.	Imper.	Aorist.
برنشستن *to ascend*	برنشین	برنشینم
بستن *to bind*	بند	بندم
پیوستن *to join*	پیوند	پیوندم
شکستن *to break*	شکن	شکنم
نشاستن *to cause to sit down*	نشان	نشانم
نشستن *to sit down*	نشین	نشینم

XI.

Irregulars that add ي.

Infin.	Imper.	Aorist.
زادن *to be born*	زاي	زايم
كادن *to caress*	كاي	كايم
كشادن *to open*	كشاي	كشايم

XII.

Irregulars that reject ادن

Infin.	Imper.	Aorist.
افتادن *to fall*	افت	افتم
ايستادن *to stand*	ايست	ايستم
فرستادن *to send*	فرست	فرستم
نهادن *to place*	نه	نهم

XIII.

Irregulars not reducible to any class.

Infin.	Imper.	Aorist.
آمادن *to prepare*	اماز	امازم
آمدن *to come*	آي	آيم
بودن *to be*	باش	باشم
خاستن *to rise*	خيز	خيزم
دادن *to give*	ده	دهم
زدن *to strike*	زن	زنم
ستدن and ستاشتن } *to take*	ستان	ستانم

Infin.	Imper.	Aorist.
سرشتن *to mix, compose*	سريش	سريشم
كردن *to do*	كن	كنم
كشستن and كسيختن } *to break*	كسيل	كسيلم
كندن *to rot*	كند	كندم
مردن *to die*	مير	ميرم
نيشتن and نوشتن } *to write*	نويس	نويسم

Example of an irregular verb.

يافتن yāfṭan, *to find*. Contracted infinitive يافت

Present Tense.

Sing.	Plur.
مي يابم *I find.*	مي يابيم *we find.*
مي يابي *thou findest.*	مي يابيد *you find.*
مي يابد *he finds.*	مي يابند *they find.*

Preterite.

يافتم *I found.*	يافتيم *we found.*
يافتي *thou foundest.*	يافتيد *you found.*
يافت *he found.*	بافتند *they found.*

Future, or Aorist.

Sing.	Plur.
يابم *I shall* or *may find.*	يابيم *we shall* or *may find.*
يابي *thou shalt* or *mayst find.*	يابيد *you shall* or *may find.*
يابم *he shall* or *may find.*	يابند *they shall* or *may find.*

Imperative.

ياب or بياب *find thou.* يابيد *find you.*

Participles.

Present, يابا, ياب, or يابنده *finding.*
Preterite, يافته *having found.*

آن به كه زصبر رخ نتابم
باشد كه مراد دل بيابم

It is better for me not to turn my face from patience; it may happen that I may find what my heart desires.

The contracted participles, as it has been before observed, are of great use in the composition of words, as عشرت انگيز *mirth-exciting*, from عشرت which in Arabic signifies *mirth*, and the participle of انگيختن *to excite*: but of these elegant compounds I shall speak at large in the next section.

OF THE COMPOSITION

AND

DERIVATION OF WORDS.

ONE of the chief beauties of the Persian language is the frequent use of compound adjectives; in the variety and elegance of which it surpasses not only the German and English, but even the Greek. These compounds may be multiplied without end according to the pleasure and taste of the writer; they are formed either by a noun and the contracted participle, as دل فریب or دلفریب *heart-alluring;* or by prefixing an adjective to a noun, as خوشبوي *sweet-smelling;* or lastly, by placing one substantive before another, as گلعذار *rose-cheeked.*

Since one of the nouns in a compound word is often borrowed from the Arabic, a man who wishes to read the Persian books with satisfaction, ought to have a competent knowledge of both languages. I shall subjoin a list of the most elegant compounds that I can recollect; but I must express most of them in English by circumlocutions: for though we have some compound epithets which give a grace to our poetry, yet in general the genius of our language seems averse to them. Thus آهو چشم from آهو *a fawn*, and چشم *an eye*, a Persian epithet, which answers to the Greek ἑλικῶπις, seems very harsh in English, if we translate it *fawn-eyed;* Lady Wortley Mountague's translation *stag-eyed* * is not much better, and conveys a different idea from what the Eastern poets mean to express by this epithet.

I.

Adjectives compounded of nouns and participles.

گل افشان gul afshān,	*shedding flowers.*
دُرّافشان durr afshān,	*sprinkling pearls.*
گوهر افشان gōḥar afshān,	*shedding gems.*
تيغ افشان ṭēgh afshān,	*brandishing a scymitar.*
خون افشان khūn afshān	*dropping blood.*
دل آزار dil āzār,	*afflicting the heart.*
جان آزار jān āzār,	*wounding the soul.*
تاب افگن ṭāb afgan,	*darting flames.*
بيخ افگن bēkh afgan,	*tearing up roots.*
سنگ افگن ṣang afgan,	*casting stones.*
كوه افگن kōḥ afgan,	*throwing down mountains.*

* See her Letters from Constantinople.

مرد افگن mard afgan, *overthrowing heroes.*
عنبر آگین ɛambar āgīn, *full of ambergris.*
سرور آگین surūr āgīn, *full of pleasures.*
مراد آور murād āwar, *fulfilling our desires.*
دل آور dil āwar, *stealing hearts.*
جهان آرا jahān ārā,
and عالم آرا ɛālam ārā, } *adorning the world.*
مجلس آرا majlis ārā, *gracing the banquet.*
دل آرا dil ārā, *rejoicing the heart.*
دل آرام dil ārām, *giving rest to the heart.*
نبرد آزما nabard āzmā, *experienced in battle.*
روح آسا rūḥ āṣā, *appeasing the spirit,*
جان آسا jān āṣā, *giving rest to the soul.*
خون آلود khūn ālūd, *sprinkled with blood.*
غبار آلود ghubār ālūd, *covered with dust.*
خطا آلود khaṭā ālūd *stained with crimes.*
روح افزا rūḥ afzā, *refreshing the spirit.*
بهجت افزا bahjat afzā, *increasing cheerfulness.*
شهر اشوب shahr ashūb, *disturbing the city;*

elegantly applied to *beauty*, to which likewise the poets give the following epithet,

روز افزون rōz afzūn, *increasing daily.*

سر افراز ṣar afrāẓ, *raising his head.*

گردن افراز gardan afrāẓ, *exalting his neck.*

عالم افروز ɛālam afrōẓ, or جهان افروز jahān afrōẓ, *enlightening the world.*

گيتي افروز gīṭī afrōẓ, *enflaming the universe.*

معركه افروز maɛrikah afrōẓ, *kindling the fight.*

بوستان افروز bōṣṭān afrōẓ, *inflaming the garden.*

a beautiful epithet for the anemone.

دانش آموز dānish āmōẓ, *skilled in science.*

كار آموز kār āmōẓ, *expert in affairs.*

مژده آمیز muĵdah āmēẓ, *mixed with joyful tidings.*

This participle آمیز is used in a great variety of compounds.

راحت آمیز rāhaṭ āmēẓ, *giving rest.*

ستم آمیز siṭam āmēẓ, *full of threats.*

شهد آمیز shahd āmēẓ, *mixed with honey.*

رنگ آمیز rang āmēẓ, *mixed with colours,* that is, deceitful.

پرتو انداز parṭō andāẓ, *darting rays.*

دهشت انداز dahshaṭ andāẓ, *striking with fear.*

آتش انداز āṭish andāẓ, *casting out fire.*

تیر انداز ṭīr andāẓ, *shooting arrows.*

ظلمت اندوز żulmaṭ andōż, *gathering darkness.*
an epithet of the night.

عبرت اندوز ѐibraṭ andōż, *attracting wonder.*

التفات انگیز iltifāṭ angēż, *exciting respect.*

خلوص انگیز khulūṣ angēż, *promoting sincerity.*

فتنه انگیز fiṭnaḥ angēż, *raising a tumult.*

خجلت انگیز khajlaṭ angēż, *causing blushes to rise.*

خفقان انگیز khafaḳān angēż, *making the heart beat.*

ارشاد انگیز irshād angēż, *producing safety.*

مردم اوبار mardam ōbār, *devouring men.*

جان افرین jān afrīn, *that created the soul.*

دل بر dil bar, *a ravisher of hearts.*

سایه پرور ṣāyaḥ parwar, *bred in the shade,*
an epithet for an ignorant young man who has not seen the world.

علما پرور ѐulamā parwar, *cherishing learned men.*

تن پرور ṭan parwar, *nourishing the body.*

عشق باز ѐishḳ bāż, *sporting with love.*

پوزش پذیر pōżīsh pażīr, *accepting an excuse.*

ترانه پرداز ṭurānaḥ pardāż, *composing tunes,*
a musician.

سخن پردز ṣakhun pardāż, *composing sentences,*
an orator.

نقل بند nakl band, *compiling narratives.*
an historian.

عدوبند ɛadū band, *that enslaves his enemies.*

فتنه بیز fitnah bēz, *spreading sedition.*

عطر بیز ɛitar bēz, *shedding perfume.*

نادره پیرا nādarah pīrā, *collecting memorable events.*

آسمان پیوند āsmān paywand, *reaching the sky.*

عالمتاب ɛālam tāb, *inflaming the world.*
an epithet of the sun.

دولتجوي dawlat jōyi, *wishing prosperity.*

گل چین gul chīn, *gathering roses.*

شگوفه چین shagūfah chīn, *cropping flowers.*

سخن چین sakhun chīn, *collecting words,*
an informer.

سحر خیز sahar khēz, *rising in the morning.*

خوشخوان khūsh kh'ān, *sweetly singing.*

جهاندار jahān dār, *possessing the world.*

نکته دان noktah dān, *skilful in subtleties.*

خرده بین khurdah bīn, *seeing minute objects.*

سخن ران sakhun rān, *lengthening his discourse.*

کامران kām rān, *gaining his desires.*

خون ریز khūn rēz, *shedding blood.*

شکرریز	shakar rēž,	*dropping sugar.*
گہرریز	gohar rēž,	*scattering jewels.*
اشک ریز	ashk rēž,	*shedding tears.*
غمزدا	gham žadā,	*dispersing care.*
ظلمت زدا	žulmaṭ žadā,	*dispelling darkness.*
رهزن	rah žan,	*infesting the way*, a robber.
سحرساز	sihr ṣāž,	*preparing inchantments.*
دلستان	dil ṣiṭān,	*ravishing hearts.*
دلسوز	dil ṣōž,	*inflaming the heart.*
جان شکار	jān shikār,	*a hunter of souls.*
عمرشکاف	ɛumr shikāf,	*destroying life.*
صف شکن	ṣaf shikan,	*breaking the ranks.*
انجم شمار	anjum shumār,	*equal to the stars in number.*
کارشناس	kār shināṣ,	*skilful in business.*
شکرفروش	shakar farōsh,	*selling sugar.*
خود فروش	khūd farōsh,	*boasting of himself.*
ناظرفریب	nāžir farēb,	*deceiving the beholder.*
جگرگداز	jigar gudāž,	*melting the heart.*
صمّاگداز	ṣummā gudāž,	*dispelling a calamity.*
ضیاگستر	žayā guṣṭar,	*spreading light.*
عالمگیر	ɛālam gīr,	*subduing the world.*
دلکشا	dil kushā,	*rejoicing the heart.*

کشورکشا kishwar kushā, *conquering provinces.*
اورنگ نشین awrang nashīn, *sitting on a throne.*
ویرانه نشین wayrānah nashīn, *inhabiting a desert.*
رهنما rah namā, *showing the way.*
غریب نواز gharīb nawāz, *kind to strangers.*
بربط نواز burbut nawāz, *tuning a lute.*
کمیاب kām yāb, *who finds what he desires.*

II.

Words compounded of adjectives and nouns.

خوب روي khūb rōyi, *with a beautiful face.*
پاکیزه خوي pākīzah khōyi, *having pure intentions.*
خوشخوي khūsh khōyi, *of a sweet disposition.*
پاکدامن pāk dāman, *with unblemished virtue.*
خوب آواز khūb āwāz, *with a good voice.*
خوب رایحه khūb rāyḥah, *with a pleasing scent.*
خوش الحان khūsh alḥān, *with sweet notes.*

an epithet of the nightingale, as in this elegant distich,

رونق عهد شبابست دگر بستانرا
میرسد مژده گل بلبل خوش الحانرا

The brightness of youth again returns to the bowers;
The rose sends joyful tidings to the nightingale with sweet notes.

خوش رفتار khūsh rafṭār, *walking gracefully.*

شيرينكار shīrīn ḳār, *with gentle manners.*

شيرين دهن shīrīn daḥan, *with a sweet mouth.*

سياه چشم ṣiyāḥ chashm, *black-eyed.*

The compounds of this form are very numerous, and may be invented at pleasure.

III.

Adjectives compounded of two nouns.

Each of these epithets is a short simile.

پري روي parī rōyi, } *with the face of an angel.*
پري پيكر parī payḳar, }

پري رخسار pari rokhṣār, *with the cheeks of an angel.*

جمشيد كلاه Jamshīd ḳulāh, *with the diadem of Gemshid.*

دارا حشمت Dārā ḥashmaṭ, *with the troops of Darius.*

سيمين ساق ṣīmīn ṣāḳ, *with legs like silver.*

شكرلب shaḳar lab, *with lips of sugar.*

طوطي گفتار ṭūṭī guftār, *talking like a parrot.*

غنچه لب ghunchah lab,	*with lips like rose-buds.*
سمن بوي ṣaman bōyi,	*with the scent of jessamine.*
سمن بر ṣaman bar,	*with a bosom like jessamine.*
گلرخ gul rōkh,	*with cheeks like roses.*
گلروي gul rōyi,	*with a rosy face.*
مشكبوي muskh bōyi,	*with the scent of musk.*
ياكوت لب yāḳūṭ lab,	*with lips like rubies.*
شيردل shēr dil,	*with the heart of a lion.*

When we consider the vast number of epithets that may be compounded after these three forms, and that those epithets are often used for substantives without a noun being expressed, we must allow that the Persian language is the richest in the world. These compounds are thought so beautiful by the Persian poets, that they sometimes fill a distich with them, as

ماهروي مشكبوي دلكشي
جانفزاي دلفريبي مهوشي

A damsel with a face like the moon, scented like musk, a ravisher of hearts, delighting the soul, seducing the senses, beautiful as the full moon.

The particle هم ḥam, *together*, prefixed to nouns, forms another elegant class of compounds implying *society* and *intimacy*, as

هماشيان ḥamāshiyān,	*of the same nest.*
هماهنگ ḥamāḥang,	*of the same inclination.*
همبزم ḥambažm,	*of the same banquet.*
همبستر ḥambiṣṭar,	*lying on the same pillow.*
همخوابه ḥamkh'ābaḥ,	*sleeping together.*
همدم ḥamdam,	*breathing together*, that is, very intimately connected.

The particles نا *not*, كم *little*, and بي *without*, are placed before nouns to denote privation, as نا اميد nā amēd, *hopeless*, نا شناس nā shanāṣ, *ignorant*, نا شگفته nā shaguftaḥ, *a rose not yet blown;* كمبها kambaḥā, *of little value*, كم عقل kam ɛakl, *with little sense;* بي باك bī bāk, *fearless*, بي امان bī amān, *merciless:* this particle is often joined to Arabic verbs, as بي تامّل bī ṭāmmul, *inconsiderate*, بي ترتيب bī ṭarṭīb, *irregular*.

Example.

بعد ازين نامترا درهر كجا خواهم نوشت

بي حقيقت بى مروت بي وفا خواهم نوشت

Henceforth, wherever I write thy name, I will write *false, unkind* and *faithless.*

Names of agents are generally participles active in نده as سازنده ṣāżandah, *a composer;* or they are formed by adding گر gar, گار gār, or بان bān to a substantive, as زرگر *a goldsmith,* قلمگار *a writer,* باغبان *a gardiner.*

Nouns of action are often the same with the third person preterite of a verb, as خرید و فروخت *buying and selling,* آمد و شد *coming and going.*

Adjectives implying possession or plenty are formed by adding to nouns the termination سار ṣār, گین gīn, مند mand, ناگ nāg, وار wār, or ور war, as شرمسار *bashful,* غمگین *sorrowful,* دانشمند *learned,* زهرناگ *venomous,* امیدوار *hopeful,* جانور *having life.*

The Arabic words ذو żū, صاحب ṣāḥib and اهل ahl prefixed to nouns form likewise abjectives of possession, as ذو جلال *majestic,* dignitate præditus, صاحب جمال *beautiful,* venustate præditus, اهل حکمت *wise,* sapientiâ præditus. We may here observe, that the Indians use a great variety of phrases purely Arabic, some as proper names and titles of chiefs and princes, and others as epithets or constant adjuncts to substantives; such are the names شجع الدّوله Shujaεud'dawlah̤, نجم الدّوله Najmud'-dawlah̤, شمس الدّوله Shamṣud'dawlah̤, سراج الدّوله Sa-rājud'dawlah̤, which signify in Arabic *the force, the star, the sun, and the lamp of the state;* such also is the title which they gave Lord Clive, زبدة الملك Zabdaṭu'lmulk̤, *the flower of the kingdom;* in the same manner they seldom mention the province of بنگاله Bangālah̤ without adding, by way of epithet, جنّت البلاد jannaṭulbalād, *the paradise of regions,* an Arabic title given to that province by آورنگ زیت Awrangžēb.

Some adjectives are formed from nouns by adding ین īn, as آتشین *fiery,* زرین *golden,* زمردین *made of emeralds.*

The termination انه anah̤ added to substantives forms adverbs that imply a kind of similitude, as دانایانه *prudently, like a prudent man,* مردانه *courageously, like a man of courage.*

Adjectives of similitude are formed by adding آسا āṣā, سا ṣā, or وش wash, to substantives, as عنبر آسا εambar āṣā, *like ambergris,* مشک آسا *like musk,* جنت آسا *like paradise;* سحر سا *like magic;* غنچه وش *like a rose-bud,* قمروش or مهوش *like the moon.*

Some adjectives and adverbs are formed by nouns doubled with the letter ا alif between them, as لبالب *up to the brim*, سراسر *from the beginning to the end*, رنگارنگ or گوناگون *many-coloured.*

Example.

روضة ماء نهرها سلسال
دوحة سجع طيرها موزون
آن پر از لالهاي رنگارنگ
وين پر از ميوهاي گوناگون

A garden, in which were the clearest rivulets, an orchard in which the notes of the birds were melodious; the one was full of *many-coloured* tulips, the other full of fruits *with various hues.*

The two first lines of this terastich are in pure Arabic.

The termination فام fām, as well as گون gūn, denotes colour, as گلفام or گلگون *rose-coloured*, زمردفام *emerald-coloured.*

From the compounds above-mentioned, or any other adjectives, compounded or simple, may be formed abstract substantives by adding ي, as

شرمسار *bashful*, شرمساري *bashfulness.*

دانشمند *learned*, دانشمندي *learning.*

سیاه *black*, سیاهي *blackness.*

If the adjective end in ه the abstract is made by changing ه into گي, as بیگانه *new*, بیگانگي *novelty.*

Other abstracts are made either by adding ار ar to the third person of the past tense, as دیدار *sight*, گفتار *speech*, رفتار *motion;* or by adding ش to the contracted participle, a اسایش *rest*, ستایش *praise*, ازمایش *temptation.*

The letter ا alif added to some adjectives makes them abstract nouns, as گرم *warm*, گرما *warmth.*

Nouns denoting the place of any thing are formed by the terminations استان istān; دان dān, زار zār, گاه gāh, or جا jā, as

نگارستان nagaristān,* *a gallery of pictures.*

* The five first of these names are the titles of as many excellent books: the *Bahāristān* and *Gulistān* are poetical compositions by *Jāmī* and *Sādī;* the *Nagāristān* is a very entertaining miscellany in prose and verse; and the *Shakardān* is a miscellaneous work in Arabic upon the history of Egypt: as to the *Sambulistān*, I have seen it quoted; but recollect neither the subject, nor the name of its author. The Greeks sometimes gave these flowery titles to their books; thus Pamphilus published a treatise on different subjects, which he called Λειμών چمنزار *a meadow;* and Apostolius compiled an Ἰωνιὰ بنفشه زار *a garden of violets*, or a collection of proverbs and sentences.

بهارستان bahāristān, *the mansion of the spring.*
گلستان gulistān, *a bower of roses.*
شکردان shakardān, or شکرستان shakaristān, *a chest of sugar.*
سنبلستان sambulistān, *a garden of hyacinths.*
شیرستان shēristān, *the country of lions.*
جنستان ginistān, *fairy-land.*
گلزار gulzār, *a bed of roses.*
لالهزار lālahzār, *a border of tulips.*
عبادتگاه ɛibādatgāh, *a place of worship.*
خواب جا khāb jā, *the place of sleep*, a bed.

The learner must remember, that when these compounds are used as distinct substantives, the termination ان of the plural, and را of the oblique case, must be added to the end of them, as

Sing. Nom. شیرین دهن } *a girl with sweet lips.*
Obl. شیرین دهنرا

Plur. Nom. شیرین دهنان } *girls with sweet lips.*
Obl. شیرین دهنانرا

The Persian verbs are compounded either with nouns and adjectives, or with prepositions and other participles.

The verbs chiefly used in the first sort of composition are کردن *to do,* آوردن *to bring,* داشتن *to have,* ساختن *to make,* فرمودن *to order,* خوردن *to devour,* زدن *to strike,* بردن *to bear,* نمودن *to show.* گشتن or گردیدن *to become,* آمدن *to come,* دیدن *to see,* گرفتن *to take,* and یافتن *to find.* The most common of these is کردن which is joined in all its inflexions to a multitude of Arabic gerunds or verbal nouns, as well as to Persian adjectives and participles, as

اقرار کردن ikrār kardan, *to confess*
انتظار کردن intizār kardan, *to expect*
رجوع کردن rujūع kardan, *to return.*
تمام کردن tamām kardan, *to complete.*
پر کردن pur kardan, *to fill.*
ترک کردن tark kardan, *to leave.*
طلوع کردن tulūع kardan, *to rise* (oriri).

Thus Hafiz,

صبحست ساقیا قدحی پر شراب کن
دور فلک درنگ ندارد شتاب کن
خورشید می ز مشرق ساغر طلوع کرد
گر برگ عیش میطلبی ترک خواب کن

It is morning; boy, *fill* the cup with wine: the rolling heaven makes no delay; therefore *hasten*. The sun of the wine *rises* from the east of the cup: if thou seekest the delights of mirth, *leave* thy sleep.

هجوم آوردن ḥujūm āwardan, *to assault.*
یاد آوردن yād āwardan, *to remember.*
عجب داشتن ʿajab dāshṭān, *to wonder.*
معذور داشتن maʿẕūr dāshṭan, *to excuse.*
حسد بردن ḥaṣad burdan, *to envy.*
اعتقاد بردن iʿṭiḳād burdan, *to believe.*
غم خوردن ghamm khūrdān, *to grieve.*
سوگند خوردن ṣōgand khūrdan, *to swear.*
روشن ساختن rōshan ṣākhṭan, *to enlighten.*
تر ساختن ṭar ṣākṭan, *to moisten.*
التفات نمودن ilṭifāṭ namūdan, *to esteem.*
مدهوش گشتن madḥōsh gashṭan, *to be astonished.*
غمناک گردیدن ghamnāg gardīdan, *to be afflicted.*
پدید آمدن padīd āmadan, *to appear.*
احسان دیدن iḥṣān dīdan, *to be benefited.*
پرورش یافتن parwarish yāfṭan, *to be educated.*
قرار گرفتن ḳarār girifṭan, *to be confirmed.*

The verbs زدن and فرمودن are very frequently used in composition, as نعره زدن naɛrah̤ žadan *to call aloud,* فکر فرمودن fik̤r farmūdan *to consider;* thus Jalāluddīn Rōžbahār,

تا بحمد تو نعره زد بلبل
همه گوشم چون درخت گل

While the nightingale sings thy praises with a loud voice,
I am all ear, like the rose-tree.

And Hafiz,

فکر معقول بفرما گل بیخار کجاست

Consider attentively; where is a rose without a thorn?

Some of the particles, with which verbs are compounded, are significant, and others rudundant and ornamental, as

درآمدن dar āmadan,	*to enter.*
درآوردن dar āwardan,	*to bring in.*
درخواستن dar kh'āṣṭān,	*to require.*
دریافتن dar yāfṭan,	*to understand.*
برآمدن bar āmadan,	*to ascend.*
برگشتن bar gashṭan,	*to return.*
برآسودن bar āṣūdan,	*to rest.*

بازداشتن bāž dāshṭan, *to with-hold.*

فرود آمدن farōd āmadan, *to descend.*

واپس داشتن wāpaṣ dāshṭan, *to detain.*

سر دادن ṣar dādan, *to banish,*to confine to a place.

In the present tense of a compound verb the particle مي is inserted between the two words of which it is composed, as پر كردن *to fill.*

Sing.	Plur.
پر مي كنم *I fill.*	پر مي كنيم *we fill.*
پر مي دني *thou fillest.*	پر مي كنيد *you fill.*
پر مي كند *he fills.*	پر مي كنند *they fill.*

Sometimes the two words of which a verb is compounded are placed at a great distance from each other, as

صبا بلطف بگو آن غزال رعنارا
كه سر بكوه و بيابان تو دادهٔ مارا

O western breeze, say thus to yon tender fawn, thou hast confined us to the hills and deserts,

where دادهٔ سر the preterite of سر دادن *to confine,* relé-guer, is separated by three words. The noun سر has a number of different senses, and is therefore the most difficult word in the Persian language; it signifies *the head, the top, the point, the principal thing, the air, desire, love, will, intention, &c.* and sometimes its meaning is so vague that it seems a mere expletive, though the Persians undoubtedly feel its force.

There are derivative verbs in Persian, as in Hebrew and Arabic, which may be called *causals;* they are formed from the transitive verbs by changing یدن into انیدن, and sometimes into ایانیدن, as

تابیدن *to shine.* تانانیدن and تابایانیدن } *to cause to shine.*

رسیدن *to arrive.* رسانیدن *to cause to arrive,* to conduct, bring.

یارب آن آهوي مشکین بختن بازرسان
وآن سهي سرو خرامان بچمن بازرسان

O heaven! *bring* that musky fawn back to Khoten; bring back that tall waving cypress to its native garden.

OF PERSIAN NUMBERS.

The numerals and invariable parts of speech belong more properly to a vocabulary than to a grammar; but for the use of such as will take the trouble to learn them by heart, I will here subjoin the most common of them:

۱	ا	یک yak	*one.*
۲	ب	دو dō,	*two.*
۳	ج	سه seh,	*three.*
۴	د	چهار chahār,	*four.*
۵	ه	پنج panj,	*five.*
۶	و	شش shash,	*six.*
۷	ز	هفت haft	*seven.*
۸	ح	هشت hasht,	*eight.*
۹	ط	نه nuh,	*nine.*
۱۰	ي	ده dah,	*ten.*
۱۱	یا	یازده yāzdah,	*eleven.*
۱۲	یب	دوازده dowāzdah,	*twelve.*
۱۳	یج	سیزده sēzdah,	*thirteen.*
۱۴	ید	چهارده chahārdah,	*fourteen.*
۱۵	یه	پانزده pānzdah,	*fifteen.*

١٦	يو	شانزده shānždaḥ,	*sixteen.*
١٧	يز	هفده ḥafdaḥ,	*seventeen.*
١٨	يح	هشده ḥashdaḥ,	*eighteen.*
١٩	يط	نوزده nī ždaḥ,	*nineteen.*
٢٠	ك	بيست bīṣṭ,	*twenty.*
٢١	كا	بيست ويك bīṣṭ wa yaḳ,	*twenty-one.*
٣٠	ل	سي ṣī,	*thirty.*
٤٠	م	چهل cheḥal,	*forty.*
٥٠	ن	پنجاه panjāḥ,	*fifty.*
٦٠	س	شست shaṣṭ,	*sixty.*
٧٠	ع	هفتاد ḥafṭād,	*seventy.*
٨٠	ف	هشتاد ḥashṭād,	*eighty.*
٩٠	ص	نود nawad,	*ninety.*
١٠٠	ق	صد ṣad,	*a hundred.*
٢٠٠	ر	دوصد dōṣad,	*two hundred.*
٣٠٠	ش	سيصد ṣēṣad,	*three hundred.*
٤٠٠	ت	چهارصد chaḥārṣad,	*four hundred.*
٥٠٠	ث	پانصد pānṣad,	*five hundred.*
٦٠٠	خ	ششصد shashṣad,	*six hundred.*
٧٠٠	ذ	هفتصد ḥaftṣad.	*seven hundred.*
٨٠٠	ض	هشتصد hashṭṣad,	*eight hundred.*
٩٠٠	ظ	نهصد nuḥṣad,	*nine hundred.*

١٠٠٠ غ هزار hazār, *a thousaud.*
١٠٠٠٠ یغ ده هزار dah hazār, *ten thousand.*
١٠٠٠٠٠ قغ صد هزار ṣad hazār, *a hundred thousand.*
or لک lak.

ORDINALS.

نخستین nukhuṣtīn, *first.*
دوم dōwum, *second.*
سیوم ṣēwum, *third.*
چهارم chahārum, *fourth.*
پنجم panjum, *fifth.*

All the other ordinals are formed in the same manner by adding م to the cardinal numbers.

ADVERBS.

بسیار biṣyār, *much.* اندک andak, *little.*
اینجا īnjā, *here.* آنجا ānjā, *there.*

جان نیز اگر فرستم آنجا
آن تحفهٔ مختصر چه باشد

If I could send my very soul *to that place*, how trifling a present would it be!

از اینجا aż īnjā, *hence*. از آنجا aż ānjā, *thence*.

اینسو īnṣū, *hither*. آنسو ānṣū, *thither*.

کجا kujā, *where* or *whither*. از کجا aż kujā, *whence*.

هر کجا که har kujā keh, *wheresoever*.

بیرون bērūn, *without*. درون darūn, or اندرون andarūn, *within*.

نوازنده بلبل بباغ اندرون
کرازنده آهو براغ اندرون

The nightingales were warbling in the garden, and the fawns were sporting on the hills.

فرو farō, or فرود farōd, *below*. بالا bālā, *above*.

ان بلا نبود که از بالا بود

That is not evil which comes from *above*.

بامداد b'amdād, سحرگاه ṣaḥargāh, or سحر ṣaḥar, *in the morning*.

شامگاه shāmgāh, *in the evening*.

دي dī, *yesterday*. فردا fardā, *to-morrow*.

پیش pēsh, *before*. پس paṣ, *after*.

اکنن aknun,	*now,*	آنگاه āngāh,	*then.*
چون chūn,	*when.*	هماندم hamāndam,	*directly.*
هرگز hargiž,	*ever.*	هرگزنه hargižnah	*never.*
هنوز hanūž,	*yet.*	بعد از آن baɛd až ān,	*afterward.*
تا ṭā,	*until.*	هميشه hamīshah,	*always.*
باري bārī,	*once.*	ديگربار dīgarbār,	*again.*
هم ham,	*also.*	نيز nīž,	*even.*

The following six adverbs are nearly synonymous, and signify, *as, like, in the same manner as;*

همچو hamchū,	همچون hamchūn.
چنين chunīn,	همچنين hamchunīn.
چنانچه chunāncheh,	چنانكه chunānkeh.
كو kū, *where?*	چرا charā *wherefore?*

چند chand, *how many?*

از بهر چه až bahr cheh, *on what account?*

چون chūn,	*how?*	چگونه chegūnah	*how,* or *what.*
اينك īnak,	*behold!*	كاش kāsh,	*would!*
مگر magar,	*perhaps.*	مبادا mabādā,	*lest by chance.*

هم ham, and بهم baham, } *together.* تنها ṭanhā, *alone.*

CONJUNCTIONS.

و ō, va, or wa, *and*. هم ẖam, or نیز nīž, *also*.

یا yā, *or*. اگر agar, or گر 'gar, *if*.

اگرچه agarcheẖ, گرچه 'garcheẖ, *though*.

امّا ammā, لیکن lēkan, بل bal, بلکه balkeẖ, *but*.

هرچند ẖarchand, هرچندکه ẖarchandkeẖ, *although*.

بنابرین banābarīn, *therefore*. پس pas, *then*, *moreover*.

که keẖ, *since*. زیرا žērā, *because*.

مگر magar, *unless*. جز juž, *except*.

PREPOSITIONS.

از až or ز 'ž, *from*, *by*, *of*. ابر abar. or بر bar, *upon*.

پس pas, *after*. پیش pēsh, *before*.

به baẖ, or ب ba, joined to the noun, *to*.

با bā, *with*. بي bī, *without*.

پهلوي paẖlawī, *near*, در dar, *in*.

براي barāy, بجهت bajeẖat, *for*.

ازجهت až jeẖat از بهر až baẖr, *on account of*.

میان miyān, *between*. سوي suwī, *toward*.

فرود farōd, *beneath*. زیر žēr, *under*.

زبر žabar, *above*. نزد nažd, *near*.

INTERJECTIONS.

ايا ayā, ايها ayḥā, *oh!*   آه āḥ!

دريغ or دريغا darēghā, *alas!*

Thus in the tale of the merchant and the parrot by Jalāluddīn Rūmī,

اي دريغا واي دريغا واي دريغ
كانچنان ماهي نهان شد زير ميغ

Alas! alas! that so bright a moon should be hidden by the clouds!

فغان fighān and افسوس afṣōṣ are likewise interjections that express grief: thus in a tetrastich by the sultan Togrul Ben Erslan,

ديروز چنان وصال جان فروزي
وامروز چنين فراق عالم سوزي
افسوس كه بر دفتر عمرم ايام
آنرا روزي نويسد اينرا روزي

Yesterday the presence of my beloved delighted my soul; and to-day her absence fills me with bitterness; alas! that the hand of fortune should write joy and grief alternately in the book of my life!

This great hero and poet was the last king of the Seljukian race; he was extremely fond of Fardōṣī's poetry, and in the battle in which he lost his life, he was heard to repeat aloud the following verses from the Shāhnāmah:

چو برخاست از لشکر کش گرد
رخ نامداران ما گشت زرد
من این گرز یکزخم برداشتم
سپه را همان جاي بگذاشتم
خروشي بر آورد اسبم چو پیل
زمین شد پریشان چو دریاي نیل *

When the dust arose from the approaching army, the cheeks of our heroes turned pale; but I raised my battle-ax, and with a single stroke opened a passage for my troops: my steed raged like a furious elephant, and the plain was agitated like the waves of the Nile.

* These lines are quoted by d'Herbelot, p. 1029, but they are written differently in my manuscript of *Fardōṣī*, which I have here followed.

OF THE PERSIAN SYNTAX.

THE construction of the Persian tongue is very easy, and may be reduced to a few rules, most of which it has in common with other languages. The nominative is usually placed before the verb, with which it agrees in number and person, as in this pious sentence of a Persian philosopher,

از بهر چه آمدهٔ اگر آمدهٔ که علم اوّلین و اخرین بیاموزي
این راه روا نیست این همه خالق داند و اگر آمدهٔ که اورا
جویي آنجاکه اوّل قیام برگرفتي او خود آنجا بود*

Wherefore *art thou come?* if *thou art come* to learn the science of ancient and modern times, thou hast not taken the right path: the *Creator knoweth* all this; and if *thou art come* to seek him, know that where *thou* first *wast fixed*, there *he was present.*

* See the Bibliotheque Orientale, p. 950.

yet it is remarkable, that many Arabic plurals are considered in Persian as nouns of the singular number, and agree as such with verbs and adjectives, as

از آمدن بهار از رفتن دي
اوراق حیات ما میگردد طي

By the approach of spring, and the return of December, the leaves of our life are continually folded.

where اوراق the plural of ورق *a leaf*, governs میگردد in the singular.

There is another strange irregularity in the Persian syntax; the cardinal numbers are usually joined to nouns and verbs in the singular, as هزار و یک روز *a thousand and one days.*

نسیم زلفت اگر بگذرد بتربت حافظ
زخاک کالبدش صد هزار لاله بر آید

If the gale shall waft the fragrance of thy locks over the tomb of Hafiz, *a hundred thousand flowers will spring* from the earth that hides his corse.

These idioms, however, are by no means natural to the Persian, but seem borrowed from the Arabs, who say الف لیلة و لیلة *a thousand and one nights.* In Arabic too a noun of the plural number, if it signify a thing without life, requires a verb in the singular, and that of the feminine gender, for the Arabic verbs have distinct genders like nouns, as

حرّت الانهار والاغصان مالت للسجود

The rivers murmured, and the branches were bent to adore their Maker.

فاضت اقداحهم كاحداقي

Their cups overflowed with wine, and my eyes with tears.

Most active verbs require the oblique case in را after them, as

اگر آن ترک شیرازي بدست ارد دل مارا
بخال هندویش بخشم سمرقند وبخارارا

If that fair damsel of Shiraz would accept my heart, I would give for the black mole on her cheek the cities of Samarcand and Bokhārā.

It has before been observed (see page 19) that the را is omitted if the noun be indefinite or general, جام پر کن *fill* a *cup*; but that it is inserted, if the thing be particular and limited, جامرا پر کرد *he filled* the *cup*; examples of this occur in almost every page.

All nouns or verbs by which any profit or acquisition is implied, govern the oblique case, as

بلي هر جاكه شود مهر آشكارا
سهارا جز نهان بودن چه يارا

Yes! whenever the sun appears, what advantage can there be to Soha,* but his being hidden?

The following remark relates to the position rather than to the syntax: in a period of two or more members, each of which might end with an auxiliary verb, the first of them commonly contains the verb, which is understood in the rest, as

مضرّت تعجيل بسيارست و منفعت صبر و سكون بيسمار

The disadvantages of haste are many, and the advantages of patience and deliberation (are) innumerable.

The adjective is placed after its substantive, and the governing noun is prefixed to that which it governs, as روي خوب *a beautiful face*, بوي گل *the scent of a rose*; but if this order be inverted a compound adjective is formed, as, خوب روي *fair-faced*, گلبوي *rose-scented*.

* Soha is the Arabic name for a very small and obscure star in the constellation of the Great Bear.

Conjunctions which express conjecture, condition, will, motive, &c. require the conjunctive or potential mood, as

گر بدانستمي که فرقت تو
اينچنين صعب باشد و دلسوز
از تو دوري نجستمي يکدم
وز تو غايب نبودمي يکروز

If I had known *that* thy absence would have been so sorrowful and afflicting, I would not have departed from thee a single day; I would not have left thee a single moment.

Prepositions and interjections are fixed to nouns in the nominative case, as

شنوده‌ام که دو کبوتر با يکديگر در آشيانه، دمساز و در کاشانه، همراز نه از غبار اغيار بر خاطر ايشان گردي و نه از محنت روزگار در دل ايشان دردي

I have heard that two doves lived together *in* one nest, and whispered their secrets *in* one chamber; the dust of jealousy had never sullied their minds, and the anguish of misfortune had never pierced their hearts.

پرده داري ميكند در قصر قيصر عنكبوت
بومي نوبت* ميزند بر گنبد افراسياب

The spider holds the veil *in* the palace of Cæsar; the owl stands sentinel *on* the watch-tower of Afrasiab.

These are the principal rules that I have collected for the Persian language; but rules alone will avail but little, unless the learner will exemplify them in his own researches: the only office of a grammarian is to open the mine of literature, but they who wish to possess the gems must endeavour to find them by their own labours.

* نوبت is an Arabic word signifying *a turn*, *a change*, *a watch*, excubiæ: hence نوبت زدن in Persian, and نوبت چالمق in Turkish, signify *to relieve the guards by the sounds of drums and trumpets.* This office is given by the poet to the owl, as that of پرده دار or chamberlain is elegantly assigned to the spider. Some copies have نوحت instead of نوبت which reading would make very good sense, but destroys the beauty of the allusion.

A PERSIAN FABLE.

باغبان و بلبل

The GARDENER and the NIGHTINGALE.

آورده‌اند که دهقاني باغي داشت خوش و خرم و بوستاني تازه‌تر از گلستان ارم هواي آن نسيم بهار را اعتدال بخشيدي و شمامهٔ ريحان روح فزايش دماغ جان را معطر ساختي

نظم

گلستاني چو گلزار جواني
دلش سيراب آب زندگاني
نواي عندليبش عشرت انگيز
نسيم عطر سايش راحت آميز

و بر يک گوشهٔ چمنش گلبني بود تازه‌تر از نهال کامراني و سرافرازتر از شاخ شجرهٔ شادماني هر صباح بر روي گلبن گل رنگين چون عذار دلفريبان نازک خوي و رخسار سمنبران ياسمين بوي بشگفتي و باغبان با آن گل رعنا عشق بازي آغاز نموده گفتي

بيت

گل بزير لب نميدانم چه ميگويد که باز
بلبلان بي نوارا در فغان مي آورد

باغبان روزي بر عادت معهود بتماشاي گل آمد بلبلي ديد نالان که روي در صحيفهء گل مي ماليد و شيرازهء جلد زرنگار اورا بمنقار تيز از يکديگر مي گسيخت

بيت

بلبل که بگل درنگرد مست شود
سر رشتهء اختيارش ازدست شود

باغبان پريشاني اوراق گل مشاهده نموده گريبان شکيباي بدست اضطراب چاک زده و دامن دلش بخار جگردوز بيقراري دراويخت روز ديگر همان حال وجود گرفت و شعلهء فراق گل

مصراع

داغ دگرش برسر آن داغ نهاد
روز سيوم بحرکت منقار بلبل

ع

گل بتاراج رفت و خار بماند
خارخاري از آن بلبل در سينهء دهقان پديد آمده دام فريبي

در راه وي نهاد و بدانه حيل اورا صيد كرده در زندان قفس محبوس ساخت بلبل بيدل طوطي وار زبان بكشاد و گفت اي عزيز مرا بچه موجب حبس كرده از چه سبب بعقوبت مي مايل شده اگر صورت بجهت استماع نغمت من كرده خود اشيانه من در بوستان تست دم سحر طربخانه من اطراف گلستان تست و اگر مغني ديگر بخيال گذرانيده مرا از ما في الضمير خود خبر ده دهقان گفت هيچ ميداني كه بروزگار مي چه كرده و مرا بمفارقت يار نازنين چند بار ازرده سزاي آن عمل بطريق مكافات همين تواند بود كه تو از دار و ديار مانده و از تفرج و تماشا مهجور شده در گوشه زندان مي زاري و من هم درد هجران كشيده و درد فراقت جانان چشيده در كلبه احزان مي نالم

بيت

بنال بلبل اگر با منت سر ياريست
كه ما دو عاشق زاريم وكار ما زاريست

بلبل گفت ازين مقام درگذر و براندیش كه من بدين مقدار جريمه كه گلي را پريشان كرده ام محبوس گشته ام تو كه دلي را پريشان مي سازي حال تو چون خواهد بود

نظم

گنبد گردنده زروي قياس
هست به نيكي و بدي حق شناس
هر كه نكوي كند آنش رسيد
وهر كه بدي كرد زيانش رسيد

اين سخن بر دل دهقان كارگر آمده بلبل‌را آزاد كرد بلبل زباني بازادي كشاد و بگفت چون با من نكوي كردي بحكم هل جزا الاحسان الا الاحسان مكافات آن بايد كرد بدان كه دز زير درخت كه ايستاده آفتابهء است پر اززر بردار و در حوايج خود صرف كن دهقان آن محل‌را بكاويد و سخن بلبل درست يافت گفت اي بلبل عجب كه آفتابهء زررا در زير زمين مي بيني و دام در زير خاك نديدي بلبل گفت تو آنرا ندانستهء كه

اذا نزل القدر بطل الحذر

ع

با قضا كارزار نتوان كرد

چون قضاي آلهي نزول يابد ديدهء بصيرت‌را نه روشني ماند و نه تدبير و خرد نفع رساند

A literal Translation of the foregoing Fable.

THE GARDENER AND THE NIGHTINGALE.

It is related that a husbandman had a sweet and pleasant orchard, and a garden more fresh than the bower of Irem. The air of it gave mildness to the gales of the spring, and the scent of its herbs that refreshed the spirits, conveyed perfume to the very soul.

VERSES.

A bower like the garden of youth, a bed of roses bathed in the waters of life; the notes of its nightingales raising delight; its fragrant gale shedding perfume.

And in one corner of his garden there was a rose-bush fresher than the shrub of desire, and more lofty than the branch of the tree of mirth. Every morning on the top of the rose-bush the roses blossomed, coloured like the cheek of heart-alluring damsels with gentle minds, and the face of lily-bosomed maids scented like jessamine. The gardener began to show an extreme fondness for these excellent roses, and said,

A DISTICH.

I know not what the rose says under his lips, that he brings back the helpless nightingales with their mournful notes.

One day the gardener according to his established custom went to view the roses; he saw a plaintive nightingale, who was rubbing his head on the leaves of the roses, and was tearing asunder with his sharp bill that volume adorned with gold.

A DISTICH.

The nightingale, if he see the rose becomes intoxicated; he lets go from his hand the reins of prudence.

The gardener viewing the scattered condition of the rose-leaves, tore with the hand of confusion the collar of patience, and rent the mantle of his heart with the piercing thorn of uneasiness. The next day he found the same action repeated, and the flames of wrath occasioned by the loss of his roses,

AN HEMISTICH.

added another scar to the scar which he had before.

The third day, by the motion of the nightingale's bill,

AN HEMISTICH.

the roses were plundered, and the thorns only remained. Then the resentment caused by the nightingale broke out in the breast of the gardener; he set a deceitful springe in his way, and having caught him with the bait of treachery, he confined him in the prison of a cage. The disheartened nightingale opened his mouth, like a parrot, and said, Oh, Sir, for what cause hast thou imprisoned me? for what reason hast thou resolved to distress me? if thou formest the desire of hearing my songs, my own nest is in thy garden, where in the morning thy bower shall be the house of my music; but if thou hast another idea, inform me of what thou hast in thy mind (an Arabic phrase).

The gardener, said, Dost thou not know how thou hast spoiled my fortune, and how often thou hast distressed me with the loss of my favourite rose? it is right that thy action should be requited, and that thou being separated from thy friends and family, and secluded from all joy and diversions, shouldst mourn in the corner of a prison; whilst I, afflicted with the anguish of separation from my darling flowers, weep in the cottage of care.

A DISTICH OF HAFIZ.

Mourn, O nightingale! if with me thou regrettest the loss of thy friend, for we are two mournful lovers, and our employment is weeping.

The nightingale said, Depart from that resolution, and consider, that if I am imprisoned for such an offence as tearing a rose, what will be thy punishment if thou tearest a heart asunder?

VERSES.

He that formed the sky by exact measure, knows the right rewards for good and evil; whoever does well, good will come to him; and if he does ill, evil will attend him.

This discourse taking effect upon the heart of the gardener, he set the nightingale at liberty. The bird tuned his voice in his free state, and said, Since thou hast done me this service, according to the sentence (in the Alcoran) Is there any recompense for benefits, but benefits? it is necessary to reward thee for it. Know, that under the tree where thou standest there is a coffer full of gold; take it, and spend it to supply thy wants.

The gardener searched the place, and found the words of the nightingale to be true; he then said, O nightingale! what a wonder it is, that thou couldst see the coffer of gold beneath the earth, and not discover the springe upon the ground!

The nightingale said, Dost thou not know that (an Arabic sentence) when fate descends, caution is vain?

An HEMISTICH.

It is impossible to contend with fate.

When the decrees of heaven are fulfilled, no light remains to the eye of understanding, and neither prudence nor wisdom bring any advantage.

عروض
OF VERSIFICATION.

THE modern Persians borrowed their poetical measures from the Arabs: they are too various and complicated to be fully explained in this Grammar; but when the learner can read the Persian poetry with tolerable ease, he may receive further information from a treatise written professedly upon versification by وهيدي Wahīdī, who was himself no contemptible poet.*

There are nineteen sorts of metre which are used by the Persians, but the most common of them are بحر رجز or the iambic measure, بحر رمل or the trochaic measure, and بحر هزج a metre that consists chiefly of those compounded feet which the ancients called Ἐπιτρίτους, and which are composed of iambic feet and spondees alternately, as *ămātōrēs pŭēllārūm.* In lyric poetry these verses are generally of twelve or sixteen syllables, as,

ببوي نافه. كاخر صبا زان طرّه بكشايد
زجعد زلف مشكينش چه تاب افتاد در دلها

* See also Dissertations on the Rhetoric, Prosody, and Rhyme of the Persians, by Francis Gladwin. Calcutta, 1798.

˘ – – –   ˘ – – –   ˘ – – –   ˘ – – –

Babō ī nā | fah̤i k̤'ākhar | ṣabā žān ṭur | rah̤ bak̤'shāyad

˘ – – –   ˘ – – –   ˘ – – –   ˘ – – –

Zajaɛdi žul | fi mushk̤īnash | cheh ṭāb ufṭād | a dar dilhā

When the zephyr disperses the fragrance of those musky locks, what ardent desire inflames the hearts of thy admirers!

They sometimes consist of fourteen syllables in this form,

– – ˘ | ˘ – – – | – – ˘ | ˘ – – –

as

تا غنچهٔ خندانت دولت بکه خواهد داد

اي شاخ گل رعنا ازبهرکه ميرويي

– – ˘ ˘ – – – – – ˘ ˘ – – –

Tā ghuncha | h̤i khandānaṭ | dawlaṭ ba | k̤eh̤ kh'āh̤ad dād

– – ˘ ˘ – – – – – ˘ ˘ – – –

Ay shākhi | guli raɛnā | až bah̤ri | k̤eh̤ mīrōyī

Ah! to whom will the smiling rose-bud of thy lips give delight? O sweet branch of a tender plant! for whose use dost thou grow?

or in this,

– – ˘ | ˘ – – ˘ | ˘ – – | ˘ – –

as

گوشم همه بر قول ي و نغمت چنگست

چشمم همه برلعل تو و گردش جامست

˘ ˘ – – ˘ ˘ – – ˘ ˘ – –

Gōsham ḥa | maḥ bar kūli | nay ō naghma | ṭi changaṣṭ

– – ˘ ˘ – – ˘ ˘ – – ˘ ˘ – –

Chashmam ḥa | maḥ bar laɛli | ṭo ō garda | shi jāmaṣṭ

My ear is continually intent upon the melody of the pipe, and the soft notes of the lute: my eye is continually fixed upon thy rubied lip, and the circling cup.

This kind of measure is not unlike that which Sappho uses in those elegant lines quoted by Hephestion,

Γλυκεῖα ματερ ὔτοι δύναμαι κρέκειν τὸν ἰςὸν

Πόθω δαμεῖσα παιδὸς βραδινὰν δι' Ἀφροδίταν.

which he scans thus,

Γλυκεῖα μᾶ | τερ, ὔτοι δύ | ναμαι κρέκειν | τὸν ἱςὸν

Πόθα δαμεῖ | σα παιδὸς βρα | δινὰν δι' Ἀ | φροδίταν.

Other lyric verses contain thirteen syllables in this form,

˘ – ˘ – | – – – | ˘ – ˘ – | – –

as

صبا نه تهنیت پیر میفروش آمد

که موسم طرب و عیش و ناز و نوش آمد

˘ – ˘ – – – – ˘ – ˘ – – –

Sabā baḥ taḥ | nīaṭi pī | ri mayfarōsh | āmad

˘ – ˘ – – – – ˘ – ˘ – – –

Keḥ mawsimi | ṭarbō ɛish | wa nāż wa nōsh | āmad

The zephyr comes to congratulate the old keeper of the banquet-house, that the season of mirth, joy, wantonness, and wine is coming.

or,

⌣ – ⌣ – | ⌣ – – | ⌣ – ⌣ – | – –

as

صبا بلطف بگو آن غزال رعنارا

که سر بکوه و بیابان تو داده مارا

⌣ – ⌣ – ⌣ – – ⌣ – ⌣ – – –

Sabā balutf | bagō ān | ghazāli raꜥ | nārā

⌣ – ⌣ – ⌣ – – ⌣ – – – –

Keh sar bakōh | wa biābān | tō dādai | mārā

This couplet has been translated in another part of the grammar. See p. 91.

The Persians sometimes use a measure consisting of trochees and spondees alternately, like these verses of Catullus and Aristophanes.

Cras amet qui nunquam amavit, quique amavit cras amet.

Ὅσις ἡμων τὰς Ἀθήνας ἐκκεκώφηκας βοῶν.

thus Hafiz,

ابر اذاري بر آمد باد نوروزي وزيد

Abar āzārī bar āmad bādi nōrōzī wazīd.

The vernal clouds appear, the gales of the pleasant season breathe.

But the most common Persian verse contains eleven syllables, as

چونکه گل رفت و گلستان درگذشت
نشنوي زان پس زبلبل سرگذشت

Chūnkeh gul raft wa gulistān darguẑasht
Nashanwī ẑān pas ẑabulbul sarguẑasht.

When the roses wither, and the bower loses its sweetness, you have no longer the tale of the nightingale.

In this last measure are written all the great Persian poems, whether upon heroic or moral subjects, as the works of Fardōsī, and of Jāmī, the Bōstān of Sādī, and the Masnavī of the excellent Jelāluddīn. This sort of verse answers to our common heroic rhyme which was brought to so high a degree of perfection by Pope, and which the English poets will do well to retain, instead of adopting the less harmonious measures of other nations.

I have dwelt the longer upon the different sorts of verses used in Persia, because there are few books or even common letters written in the Persian language, which are not interspersed with fragments of poetry; and because all the Persian verses must be read according to the pauses of scansion: thus the following elegant couplet quoted by Meninski,

تبا در چين هر تاري بود زلف ترا صد چين
كه ساري بر گل سوري زسنبل پوده چين بر چين

must be pronounced,

Tabādar chī | na ḥar ṭārī | būwad žulfi | ṭarā ṣad chīn
Keh̤ ṣāžī bar | guli sūrī | žaṣumbul pū | dah̤ chīn bar chīn

with a strong accent upon every fourth syllable; and it may here be observed, that the Persians like the French, usually accent the last syllables of their words.

As to their prosody, nothing can be more easy and simple; their vowels ا alif, و wāw, and ي yā, are long by nature; the points, or signs for these short vowels which they commonly suppress, are naturally short; and every short syllable that ends with a consonant is long by position; as شيراز Shīrāž, سنبل ṣūmbūl, دهان dăh̤ān, سمن ṣăman: but the Persians, like other poets, have many licenses;

they often add a vowel which does not properly belong to the word, as in the first ode of Hafiz,

ولي افتاد مشكلها walī ufṭāda mushḳilḥā,

and كجا دانند حال ما kujā dānandi ḥāli mā.

They also shorten some long syllables at pleasure by omitting the vowels ا alif, و wāw, and ي yā; thus بيرون bērūn, which is a spondee, becomes an iambic foot when it is written برون bĕrūn: in the same manner دگر is used for ديگر and بدن for بودن. The omission of ا alif is more common; so ره is put for راه, and فشان for افشان, as in this beautiful couplet,

مي خواه وگلفشان كن ازدهر چه ميجويي
اين گفت سحرگه گل بلبل تو چه ميگويي

"Call for wine, and scatter flowers around; what favour "canst thou expect from fortune?" so spake the rose this morning; O nightingale! what sayst thou to her maxim?

In which lines گلفشان is used for گلافشان *shedding flowers*, and سحرگه for سحرگاه *the morning*.

I shall close this section with some examples of Persian verses from the مصراع or *hemistich*, to the غزل or *ode*, which differs from the قصيده or *elegy* in nothing but the number of the distichs, of which the ode seldom contains fewer than five, and the elegy seldom fewer than twenty. I shall not set down these examples at random, but shall select such as are remarkable for beauty of sentiment or delicacy of expression.

مصراع AN HEMISTICH.

گل نچيند كسي كه كارد خار

He who plants thorns will not gather roses.

بيت A DISTICH.

كاروان رفت و تو در خواب و بيابان در پيش
كجا روي ره زكه پرسي چكني چون باشي

The caravan is departed, and thou sleepest; the desert lies before thee; whither wilt thou go? of whom wilt thou ask the way? what wilt thou do? how wilt thou exist?

رباعي A TETRASTICH.

هنگام سپيده دم خروش سحري
داني زچه رو همي كند نوحه گري
يعني كه نمودند در آينهٔ صبح
كز عمر شبي گذشت و تو بيخبري

At the time that the dawn appears, dost thou know for what reason the bird of the morning complains? He says, that it is shown in the mirror of the day, that a whole night of thy life is passed, while thou art lost in indolence.

Another.

خواهي كه نباشي بغم رنج قرين
بشنو سخن پاكتر از دُرّ ثمين
از دشمن آزرده تغافل منماي
وزصاحب كبر و كينه ايمن منشين

Dost thou desire to be free from sorrow and pain? hear a maxim more valuable than a precious gem: Despise not thine enemy, though he be distressed; and trust not thy friend, if he be proud and malevolent.

In all the Persian elegies and odes the two first hemistichs have the same rhyme, which is continued through the whole poem at the end of every distich. A short piece of poetry, in which the two first lines do not rhyme together is called قطعة *a fragment;* as this elegant fable of Sādī on the advantages of good company,

گلي خوشبوي در حمام روزي
رسيد از دست محبوبي بدستم
بدو گفتم كه مشكي يا عنبري
كه از بوي دلاويز تو مستم
بگفتا من گلي نا چيز بودم
وليكن مدتي با گل نشستم
كمال همنشين در من اثر كرد
وگرنه من همان خاكم كه هستم

One day, as I was in the bath, a friend of mine put into my hand a piece of scented clay.* I took it, and said to it, "Art thou musk or ambergris? for I am charmed "with thy delightful scent." It answered, "I was a de- "spicable piece of clay; but I was some time in the

* گل خوشبوي gili khūshbō ī, a kind of *unctuous clay*, which the Persians perfume with essence of roses, and use in the baths instead of soap.

"company of the rose; the sweet quality of my com-
"panion was communicated to me; otherwise I should
"have been only a piece of earth, as I appear to be."

When both lines of each couplet rhyme together through a whole composition, it is called مثنوي, as in the following examples:

چنین است آیین گردنده دهر
نه لطفش بود پایدار و نه قهر
نه پرورد کس را که آخر نکشت
که در مهر نرم است و در کین درشت

Such is the nature of inconstant fortune, neither her mildness nor her violence are of long duration: she exalts no one whom she does not at last oppress; for she is light in her affection, but most harsh in her hatred.

فریدون فرّخ فرشته نبود
زمشک و زعنبر سرشته نبود
بداد و دهش یافت آن نیکویي
تو داد و دهش کن فریدون تویي

The happy Feridun * was not an angel! he was not formed

* An ancient king of Persia, highly celebrated for his eminent virtues. The learned and excellent d'Herbelot has made a mistake in his translation of these lines

of musk or ambergris. He gained his reputation by justice and liberality: be thou just and liberal, and thou wilt be a Feridun.

جواني پاکباز و پاکرو بود
که با پاکیزه رویي در گرو بود
چنین خواندم که در دریاي اعظم
بگردابي درافتادند باهم
چو ملاح آمدش تا دست گیرد
مبادا کاندرآن سختي بمیرد
همي گفت از میان موج تشویر
مرا بگذار و دست یار من گیر
درین گفتن جهان بروي دراشفت
شنیدندش که جان مي داد و مي گفت
حدیث عشق از آن بطال منیوش
که در سختي کند یار فراموش

There was an affectionate and amiable youth, who was betrothed to a beautiful girl. I have read, that as they were sailing in the great sea, they fell together into

(see the article Farrakh in his Bibliotheque Orientale); for not recollecting the sense of فرّخ HAPPY, he made a proper name of it, and tells us that Farrakh was a man whom the Persians consider as a perfect model of justice and magnanimity.

a whirlpool. When a mariner went to the young man that he might catch his hand, and save him from perishing in that unhappy juncture; he called aloud, and pointed to his mistress from the midst of the waves; "Leave me, and take the hand of my beloved." The whole world admired him for that speech; and when he was expiring he was heard to say, "Learn not the "tale of love from that wretch who forgets his beloved "in the hour of danger."

These examples will, I hope, be sufficient to undeceive those who think that the Asiatic poetry consists merely in lofty figures and flowery descriptions. There is scarce a lesson of morality or a tender sentiment in any European language, to which a parallel may not be brought from the poets of Asia. The verses of eleven syllables, which are used in the great Persian poems, always rhyme together in couplets. It is unnecessary in this section to give an example of the Persian قصيده or *elegy*, as it differs only in its length from the غزل or *ode*, except that the Kaṣṣīdaḥ often turns upon lofty subjects, and the Ghažal comprises for the most part the praises of love and merriment, like the lighter odes of Horace and Anacreon. The most elegant composers of these odes are جامي Jāmī and حافظ Hāfiẓ, each of whom has left an ample collection of his lyric poems. I may confidently affirm that few odes of the Greeks or Romans upon similar subjects are more finely polished than the songs of these Persian poets: they want only a reader that can see them in their original dress, and feel their beauties without the disadvantage of a translation. I shall transcribe the first ode of Hāfiz that offers itself, out of near three hundred that I have paraphrased: when the learner is able to understand the images and allusions in the Persian poems, he will see a reason in every line why they cannot be translated literally into any European language.

گل بي رخ يار خوش نباشد
بي باده بهار خوش نباشد
طرف چمن و طواف بستان
بي صوت هزار خوش نباشد
رقصيدن سرو و حالت گل
بي لاله عذار خوش نباشد
با يار شكرلب گلاندام
بي بوس و كنار خوش نباشد

باغ گل و ملّ خوشست امّا
بی صحبت یار خوش نباشد
هر نقش که دست عقل بندد
بي نقش و نگار خوش نباشد
جان نقد محقّرست حافظ
از بهر نثار خوش نباشد

The rose is not sweet without the cheek of my beloved; the spring is not sweet without wine.

The borders of the bower, and the walks of the garden are not pleasant without the notes of the nightingale.

The motion of the dancing cypress and of the waving flowers is not agreeable without a mistress whose cheeks are like tulips.

The presence of a damsel with sweet lips and a rosy complexion is not delightful without kisses and dalliance.

The rose-garden and the wine are sweet, but they are not really charming without the company of my beloved.

All the pictures that the hand of art can devise are not agreeable without the brighter hues of a beautiful girl.

Thy life, O Hafiz, is a trifling piece of money, it is not valuable enough to be thrown away at our feast.

The last distich alludes to the Asiatic custom of throwing money among the guests at a bridal feast, or upon any other extraordinary occasion: the Persians call this money نثار nisār, and him who collects it نثار چین nisār chīn.

I shall conclude this grammar with a translation of the ode quoted in the section upon the Persian letters; see p. 13.

If that lovely maid of Shiraz would accept my heart, I would give for the mole on her cheek the cities of Samarcand and Bokhara.

Boy, bring me the wine that remains, for thou wilt not find in paradise the sweet banks of our Rocnabad, or the rosy bowers of our Mosellâ.

Alas! these wanton nymphs, these fair deceivers, whose beauty raises a tumult in our city, rob my heart of rest and patience, like the Turks that are seizing their plunder.

Yet the charms of our darlings have no need of our imperfect love; what occasion has a face naturally lovely for perfumes, paint, and artificial ornaments?

Talk to me of the singers, and of wine, and seek not to disclose the secrets of futurity; for no one, however wise, ever has discovered, or ever will discover them.

I can easily conceive how the inchanting beauties of Joseph affected Zoleikha so deeply, that her love tore the veil of her chastity.

Attend, O my soul! to prudent counsels; for youths of a good disposition love the advice of the aged better than their own souls.

Thou hast spoken ill of me; yet I am not offended: may heaven forgive thee! thou hast spoken well: but do bitter words become a lip like a ruby, which ought to shed nothing but sweetness?

O Hafiz! when thou composest verses, thou seemest to make a string of pearls: come sing them sweetly; for heaven seems to have shed on thy poetry the clearness and beauty of the Pleïads.

The wildness and simplicity of this Persian song pleased me so much, that I have attempted to translate it in verse: the reader will excuse the singularity of the measure which I have used, if he considers the difficulty of bringing so many Eastern proper names into our stanzas.

I have endeavoured, as far as I was able, to give my translation the easy turn of the original; and I have, as nearly as possible, imitated the cadence and accent of the Persian measure; from which every reader, who understands music, will perceive that the Asiatic numbers are capable of as regular a melody as any air in Metastasio.

A PERSIAN SONG.

Sweet maid, if thou wouldst charm my sight,
And bid these arms thy neck infold;
That rosy cheek, that lily hand
Would give thy poet more delight
Than all Bocára's vaunted gold,
Than all the gems of Samarcand.

Boy, let yon* liquid ruby flow,
And bid thy pensive heart be glad,
Whate'er the frowning zealots say:
Tell them their Eden cannot show
A stream so clear as Rocnabad,
A bow'r so sweet as Moselláy.

Oh! when these fair, perfidious maids,
Whose eyes our secret haunts infest,
Their dear destructive charms display,
Each glance my tender breast invades,
And robs my wounded soul of rest,
As Tartars seize their destin'd prey.

In vain with love our bosoms glow;
Can all our tears, can all our sighs
New lustre to those charms impart?
Can cheeks where living roses blow,
Where nature spreads her richest dies,
Require the borrow'd gloss of art?

* لعل مذاب a *melted ruby* is a common periphrasis for wine in the Persian poetry. See Hafiz, ode 22.

Speak not of fate—ah! change the theme,
And talk of odours, talk of wine,
Talk of the flow'rs that round us bloom;
'Tis all a cloud, 'tis all a dream;
To love and joy thy thoughts confine,
Nor hope to pierce the sacred gloom.

Beauty has such resistless pow'r,
That e'en the chaste Egyptian dame*
Sigh'd for the blooming Hebrew boy:
For her how fatal was the hour,
When to the banks of Nilus came
† A youth so lovely and so coy!

But ah! sweet maid, my counsel hear
(Youth should attend when those advise
Whom long experience renders sage);
While music charms the ravish'd ear,
While sparkling cups delight our eyes,
Be gay; and scorn the frowns of age.

* Zoleika, Potiphar's wife. † Joseph.

What cruel answer have I heard!
And yet by heav'n, I love thee still:
Can aught be cruel from thy lip?
Yet say, how fell that bitter word
From lips which streams of sweetness fill,
Which nought but drops of honey sip?

Go boldly forth, my simple lay,
Whose accents flow with artless ease,
Like orient pearls at random strung;
Thy notes are sweet, the damsels say,
But oh, far sweeter, if they please
The nymph for whom these notes are sung!

END OF THE GRAMMAR.

A

CATALOGUE

OF THE

MOST VALUABLE BOOKS IN THE PERSIAN LANGUAGE.

Oxf. The Public Libraries at Oxford.

Par. The Royal Library at Paris.

Lond. The British Museum at London.

Priv. The Collections of private Men.

HISTORY.

كتاب روضه الصّفا تصنيف امير خوانداشاه

The garden of purity, by Mirkhond.—A general history of Persia in several large volumes. *Oxf. Priv.*

اکبرنامه ابو فضل

The history of the life of Sultan Acber, by the learned and elegant Abu Fazl. *Oxf.*

كتاب آيين اكبري

A description of the Indian empire, written by the order of Sultan Acber by a society of skilful men.—A translation of this book would be extremely useful to the European companies that trade in India, as it contains a full account of every province and city in the dominions of the Mogul, of his revenues and expences, both in peace and war, and of all the customs and ceremonies in his palace; together with a description of the natural productions of his empire. *Oxf.**

واقعات بابري

The actions of Sultan Baber; written either by himself, or under his inspection.—This book contains a minute account of that prince's wars, and a natural history of his dominions. *Oxf.*

تاريخ كشمير

The history of Chashmir, by a native of that extraordinary country.—A very curious and entertaining work. *Oxf.*

* It has since been translated into English by Francis Gladwin, Esq. originally published at Calcutta, in 3 vols. 4to

تاريخ عالم اراي عباسي

The history of the lives of the Persian kings, from the head of the Sefi family to the death of Abbas the Cruel, improperly called the Great. *Oxf.*

تاريخ گزيده

The select chronicle.—This work is an excellent history of Persia, and has been translated into Arabic and Turkish. *Oxf.*

خلاصة الاخبار

A short history of Persia, in one volume, by Khandemir, a learned and agreeable writer. *Oxf.*

لبّ التواريخ

The heart of histories. — A copious history of the Persian empire, written in the middle of the sixteenth century by Abdallatif, a native of Cazvin.

ظفر نامه

The book of victory.—A history of the life of Timur, commonly called Tamerlane, written in a most beautiful and elegant style.

تذكرة الشّعراُ تصنيف دولت شاه

An account of the lives of the Persian poets, by Dawlatshah of Samarcand. *Par.*

تاريخ جهانكشا يا تاريخ نادري من كلام ميرزا مهدي

The history of the life of Nader Shah, king of Persia, written by Mirza Mahadi, and translated into French by the author of this grammar.

POETRY.

شاه نامه فردوسي

Shah nâmeh. A collection of heroic poems on the ancient histories of Persia, by Ferdusi. See the treatise on Oriental poetry added to the life of Nader Shah, sect. II. p. 248. *Oxf. Priv.*

كليات خاقاني

The works of Khakáni, a sublime and spirited poet. *Oxf. Priv*

دیوان حافظ

The odes of Hafiz: see the treatise above-mentioned. *Lond. Oxf. Par. Priv.*

كليات سعدي

The words of Sadi: containing گلستان or *the bed of roses,* بوستان or *the garden,* and ملمعات or *the rays of light.* The two first of these excellent books are very common; but I have not seen the last: they are all upon moral subjects, and are written with all the elegance of the Persian language. *Oxf.*

كليات اهلي

The works of Ahli; containing,

سحر حلال *lawful magic,* a poem.
شمع و پروانه *the taper and the moth,* a poem.
کتاب قصاید *a book of elegies.*
کتاب غزلیات *a book of odes.*

كليات جامي

The works of Jami; containing among others,

سلسلة الذهب *the chain of gold,* a poem in three books.

قصه سلمان و ابسال *Selma and Absel*, a tale.

سکندر نامه *the life of Alexander.*

یوسف و زلیخا *the loves of Joseph and Zuleikha*, a very beautiful poem.

ليلي و مجنون *the loves of Leila and Magenun.*

ديوان جامي *a collection of odes.*

بهارستان *the mansion of the spring.*

تحفة الاحرار *the gift of the noble*

سبحة الابرار *the manners of the just.* *Oxf.*

ديوان خسرو

A book of elegant odes, by Mir Khosru. *Oxf.*

مثنوي

تصنيف جلال الدين رومي

A poetical work called *Mesnavi*, upon several subjects of religion, history, morality, and politics; composed by Geláleddin, surnamed Rúmi.—This poem is greatly admired in Persia, and it really deserves admiration. *Oxf. Priv.*

ديوان انواري

The poems of Anvári, which are quoted by Sadi in his Gulistán, and are much esteemed in the East.

كليات نظامي

The works ef Nezámi; containing six poems:

اسرار العاشقين *the secrets of lovers.*
هفت پيكر *the seven faces.*
خسرو و شيرين *the loves of Cosru and Shirin.*
سكندر نامه *the life of Alexander.*
ليلي و مجنون *Leila and Magenum,* a tale.
مخزن الاسرار *the treasure of secrets. Lond. Priv.*

پند نامه

Pendnáma, a book of moral sentences, not unlike those of Theogenis in Greek, by فريدالدين عطار Ferideddin Attar. *Lond. Oxf.*

كليات كاتبي

The works of Catebi; containing five poems:

مجمع البحرين *the junction of two seas.*
ده باب *the ten chapters.*
حسن و عشق *beauty and love.*
ناصر و منصور *the conqueror and triumpher.*
بهرام و گلاندام *the loves of Baharam and Gulendam.*

There are many more historics and poems written in Persian; but those above-mentioned are the most celebrated in Asia. The poets of the second class were رودكي Roudeki, who translated Pilpai's fables into verse; رشيدي Reshídi, who wrote an art of poetry called حدايق السحر *the inchanted gardens;* احمدي Ahmedi, who composed an heroic poem on the actions of Tamerlane: not to mention a great number of elegiac and lyric poets, who are very little known in Europe.

PHILOSOPHY.

انوار سهيلي كاشفي

The light of Soleil or canopus.—A very elegant paraphrase of Pilpai's tales and fables, by Cashefi. *Oxf.*

عيار دانش

The touchstone of learning; a more simple translation of Pilpai, by Abu Fazl. *Oxf.*

هزار يک روز

The Persian tales of a thousand and one days, translated into French by Petit de la Croix.

نگارستان جويني

Negaristáń, *the gallery of pictures*, by Jouîni.—A miscellaneous work upon moral subjects, in prose and verse. There is a beautiful copy of this book in the Bodleian library at Oxford. *Marsh* 397.

دانش نامه

A system of natural philosophy, by Isfahani. *Oxf.*

جواهر نامه

The natural history of precious stones. *Oxf.*

There are many books in Persian upon Geometry, Algebra, Astronomy, Mechanics, Logic, Rhetoric, and Physic; all which deserve to be read and studied by the Europeans. The Persians are very fond of elegant manuscripts; all their favourite works are generally written upon fine silky paper, the ground of which is often powdered with gold or silver dust: the two first leaves are commonly illuminated, and the whole book is sometimes perfumed with essence of roses or sandal wood. The poem of Joseph and Zuleikha in the public library at Oxford is, perhaps, the most beautiful manuscript in the world: the margins of every page are gilt and adorned with garlands of flowers; and the hand writing is elegant to the highest degree: it is in the collection of the learned Greaves, No. I. The Asiatics have many advantages in writing: their ink is extremely black, and never loses its colour; the Egyptian reeds with which they write, are formed to make the finest strokes and flourishes; and their letters run so easily into one another, that they can write faster than any other nation. It is not strange, therefore, that they prefer their manuscripts to our best printed books; and if they should ever adopt the art of printing, in order to promote the general circulation of learning, they will still do right to preserve their classical works in manuscript.

I shall conclude with a Persian ode in three Asiatic hands, and shall add a few remarks upon each of them.

I.

NISKHI.

This is the only form of writing that we can imitate exactly by our types:* it is the hand of the Arabians, who invented the characters; and it must, therefore, be learned before we attempt to read the other hands; it is frequently used by the Persians, and the history of Nader Shah was written in it.

II.

TALIK.

This beautiful hand may easily be read by Europeans, if they understand the Persian language; and if they do not, what will it avail them to read it? In this form of writing the strokes are extremely fine, and the initial letters ن ت ب are sometimes scarcely perceptible. The characters are the same with (or rather only a variety of) those used in

* Types have since been made in India to imitate the Talik with tolerable success; though it must be confessed, the Niskhi being the plainest, and easiest character to read, should be preferred for printing. See FORMS OF HERKERN, Calcutta, 1781.

printing, except that س and ش are often expressed by a long stroke of the reed. As the Persians always write their lines of an equal length, they are obliged to place the words in a very irregular manner; if the line be too short, they lengthen it by a fine stroke of the reed; if too long, they write the words one above another. In the Persian poems the transcribers place both members of a couplet on the same line, and not the first above the second, as we do; a Persian would write the following verses in this order,

With ravished ears	*The monarch hears,*
Assumes the god,	*Affects to nod.*

It must be confessed, that this irregularity in writing, joined to the confusion of the diacritical points, which are often placed at random, and sometimes omitted, makes it very difficult to read the Persian manuscripts, till the language becomes familiar to us; but this difficulty, like all others in the world, will be insensibly surmounted by the habit of industry and perseverance, without which no great design was ever accomplished.

III.

SHEKESTEH.

In this inelegant hand all order and analogy are neglected; the points which distinguish ف from ق, خ from ح and چ, and ب from ت, ث and پ, &c. are for the most part omitted, and these seven letters, ا د ذ ر ز ژ و are connected with those that follow them in a most irregular manner. This is, certainly, a considerable difficulty, which must be surmounted before the learner can translate a Persian letter: but I am persuaded, that those who chiefly complain of it have another difficulty still greater, which is their imperfect knowledge of the language.

NISKHI.

چو آفتاب مي از مشرق پياله برآيد
زباغ عارض ساقي هزار لاله برآيد

نسيم در بر گل بشکند کلالهٔ سنبل
چو از ميان چمن بوي آن کلاله برآيد

شکايت شب هجران نه آن شکايتهاست
که شمهٔ زبانش بصد رساله برآيد

گرت چو نوح نبي صبر هست در غم طوفان
بلا بگردد و کام هزار ساله برآيد

بسعي خود نتوان برد گوهر مقصود
خيال تست که اين کار بيحواله برآيد

زگرد خوان فلک گو طمع چه ميداري
که بيملالت صد غصه يکنواله برآيد

نسيم زلفت اگر بگذرد بتربت حافظ
زخاک کالبدش صد هزار لاله برآيد

Taleek.	*Shekesteh.*
چو آفتاب می از مشرق پیاله برآید	چو آفتاب می از مشرق پیاله برآید
ز باغ عارض ساقی هزار لاله برآید	ز باغ عارض ساقی هزار لاله برآید
نسیم در سر گل بشکند کلاله سنبل	نسیم در سر گل بشکند کلاله سنبل
چو از میان چمن بوی آن کلاله برآید	چو از میان چمن بوی آن کلاله برآید
شکایت شب هجران نه آنچنان حکایت حالیست	شکایت شب هجران نه آنچنان حکایت حالیست
که شمه‌ای ز بیانش به صد رساله برآید	که شمه‌ای ز بیانش به صد رساله برآید
گرت چو نوح نبی صبر هست در غم طوفان	گرت چو نوح نبی صبر هست در غم طوفان
بلا بگردد و کام هزار ساله برآید	بلا بگردد و کام هزار ساله برآید
به سعی خود نتوان برد پی به گوهر مقصود	به سعی خود نتوان برد پی به گوهر مقصود
خیال باشد کاین کار بی حواله برآید	خیال باشد کاین کار بی حواله برآید
ز گرد خوان نگون فلک طمع چه داری	ز گرد خوان نگون فلک طمع چه داری
که بی ملالت صد غصه یک نواله برآید	که بی ملالت صد غصه یک نواله برآید
نسیم زلف تو چون بگذرد به تربت حافظ	نسیم زلف تو چون بگذرد به تربت حافظ
ز خاک کالبدش صد هزار لاله برآید	ز خاک کالبدش صد هزار لاله برآید

An Extract from the Memoirs of the Emperor Jahāngīr, *written by Himself.*

ازعنایات بیغایات الهي یکساعت نجومي از روز پنجشنبه جمادي الثّاني هزار و چهارده هجري گذشته در دار الخلافه اگره درسنّ سي و هشت سالگي بر تخت سلطنت جلوس نمودم پدرمرا تا بیست و هشت سالگي فرزند نمیزیست و همیشه بجهت بقاي فرزند بدرویشان و گوشه نشینان که ایشان را قرب روحاني بدرگاه الهي حاصل است التجا میبردند خواجه بزرگوار خواجه معین الدّین چشتي سرچشمه اکثر اولیاي هند بودند بخاطرگذرانیدند که بجهت حصول این مطلب رجوع باستانه متبّرکه ایشان نمایند و با خود قرارداده ند ک اگر اللّه تعالي پسري کرامت فرماید و اورا بمن ارزاني دارد از اگره تاروضه منوّره ایشان که یکصد و چهل کروه است پیاده از روي نیازتمام متوجّه کردم درسه نهصد و هفتاد و هفت در روز چهارشنبه هفدهم ماه ربیع الاوّل هفت گري از روزمذکورگذشته بطالع بیست و چهارم درجه میزان اللّه تعالي مرا از کتم عدم بوجود آورد و در آن ایّام که والد بزرگوارم جویاي فرزند بودند شیخ سلیم نام درویشي صاحب حالت که طيّ سپاري از مراحل عمر نموده بود درکوهي متصل موضع سیکري که از مواضع اگره است بسرمیبرد و مردم آن نواحي شیخ اعتقاد تمام داشتند چون پدرم بدرویشان نیازمند بودند صحبت ایشان نیز دریافته روزي در اثناي توجه و بیخودي از ایشان پرسیدند که مرا چند پسرخواهد شد فرمود که بخشنده بیمنت سه پسر بشما ارزاني خواهد داشت پدرم میفرمایند که نذر نمودم که فرزند اوّل را بدامن تربیت و

توجّه شما انداخته شفقت و مهرباني شمارا حامي و حافظ اوسازم شيخ اين معني قبول ميفرمايند و بزبان ميكذرانند كه مبارك باشد ماهم ايشانرا هم نام خود ساختيم چون والدهٔ مرا هنگام وضع حمل نزديك ميرسد بخانهٔ شيخ ميفرستند تا ولادت من در انجا واقع گردد بعد از تولّد مرا سلطان سليم نام نهادند امّا من از زبان مبارك پدر خود نه در مستي و نه در هشياري هرگز نشنيدم كه مرا محمّد سليم يا سلطان سليم مخاطب ساخته باشند همه وقت شيخو بابا گفته سخن ميكردند والد بزرگوارم موضع سيكريرا كه محلّ ولادت من بود بر خود مبارك داشتند پاي تخت ساخته در عرض چهاردهٔ پانزده سال اين كوه پرجنگل پردد و دام شهري شد مشتمل بر انواع عمارات و باغات و منازل نزه و جاهاي خوش دلكش بعد ازفتح گجرات اين موضع بفتحپور موسوم گشت چو پادشاه شدم بخاطررسيد كه نام خود تغير بايد داد كه اين اسم محلّ اشتبا هست بنام قياصره روم ملهم غيب درخاطر انداخت كه كار پادشاهان جهان گيريست خودرا جهان‌گير نام نهاده و لقب خودرا چون جلوس دروقت طلوع حضرت نيّراعظم و نوراني گشتن عالم واقع شد نورالدّين سازم و درايام شهزادگي نيز از دانايان هند شنيده‌بودم كه بعد از گذشتن عهد سلطنت و زمان جلال الدّين محمّد اكبر پادشاه نورالدين نامي متقلّد امر سلطنت خواهدگشت اين معني نيز درخاتر بوده بنابرين مقدمات نورالدّين محمّدجهانگير اسم ولقب خود ساختم

A Description of the City of Agra, from the same.

اگره از شهرهاي قديم کلان هندوستانست بر کنار درياي جمنه قلعهء کهنه داشت پدرم پيش از تولد من آنرا انداخته قلعهء از سنگ سرخ تراشيده بنا نهادند که روندهاي عالم مثل اين قلعه نشان نميدهند در عرض پانزده شانزده سال باتمام رسيد مشتمل بر چهار دروازه و دو دريچه سي و پنج لک روپيه که يکصد و پانزده هزار تومار رايج ايران و يک کرور و پنج لک خاني بحساب توران خرج اين معموره بر هر دو طرف درياي مذکور واقع شده جانب غروب رويه که کثرت و اباداني بيشتر دارد و دور آن هفت کرو هست طول دو کروه و عرض يک کروه و دور ابادي آن طرف آب که بر جانب شرقي واقعست دو نيم کروه طول يک کروه و عرض نيم کروه اما کثرت عمارت بنوعيست که مثل شهرهاي عراق و خراسان و ماوراالنهر چند شهر آباد تواند شد اکثر مردم سه طبقه و چهار طبقه عمارت کرده اند و انبوهي خلق بحديست که در کوچه و بازار بدشواري تردد توان نمود از اواخر اقليم ثانيست شرقي آن ولايت قنوج و غربي تاکور و شمالي سنبل و جنوبي چنديريست در کتب هند مسطور است که منبع درياي جمنه کوهيست کلند نام که مردم را از شدت سردي عبور بر انجا ممکن نيست جايي که ظاهر ميشود کوهيست قريب بپرگنه خضرآباد هواي اگره گرم و خوشکست سخن اطبا آنست که روح را بتحليل ميبرد و ضعف مي آورد و با اکثر طبايع ناسازکار است مگر بلغمي و

سودائي مزاجان را که از ضرر آن ایمنند و ازین جهتست که حیواناتي که این مزاج و طبیعت دارند مثل فیل و گاومیش و غیر آن در این آب و هوا خوب میشوند پیش از حکومت افغانان لودي اگره معمورهٔ کلان بود ده قلعه داشت چنانکه مسعود سعد سلمان در قصیدهٔ بمدح محمود پسر سلطان ابراهیم بن مسعود بن سلطان محمود غزنوي در فتح قلعهٔ مذکور املا نموده مذکور ساخته است

بیت

حصار اگره چو پیدا شد از میانه گرد
بسان کوه و بر و بارهاي چون کهسار

چون سکندر لودي ارادهٔ گرفتن گوالیار داشت از دهلي که پاي تخت سلاطین هند است باگره آمده جاي بودن خود آنجا قرار داد از آن تاریخ اباداني و معموري اگره روي در ترقي نهاد و پاي تخت سلاطین دهلي گشت چون حضرت حق سبحانه و تعالي پادشاهي هند باین سلسلهٔ والا کرامت فرمود حضرت فردوس مکاني بابر پادشاه بعد از شکست دادن ابراهیم ولد سکندر لودي و کشته شدن او و فتح شدن رانا سانکا که کلانترین راجها و زمینداران ولایت هندوستان بود بر طرف شرقي آب جمنه زمین خوش کرده چهار باغي احداث فرمودند که در کم جاي بان لطافت باغي بوده باشد نام آن گل افشان فرمودند عمارت مختصري از سنگ تراشیده ساخته اند و مسجدي بر یک جانب آن باغ باتمام رسیده در خاطر داشتند که عمارات عالي بسازند چون عمر وفا نکرد از قوة بفعل نیامد

ADVERTISEMENT.

THE following Index will be found, it is hoped, of considerable use to learners, and to those in particular who are unprovided with dictionaries. It is not only intended as a literal alphabetical explanation and analysis of the extracts and authorities from the various writers interspersed through the Grammar, but as a vocabulary, which may be employed to advantage, by imprinting on the memory a number of useful words.

It may not be improper however to inform those who have made but little progress in this language, that in consulting any dictionary, there is a variety of inseparable particles prefixed and annexed to words, which must be analysed or separated before the meaning can be found: for example,

بکامست *which literally signifies* to desire is, *must not be looked for under the letter* ب, *but under* ک. *the* ب *prefixed being the inseparable preposition,* for, to, in, كام *implying* desire, &c. *and* ست *(for* است) *the third person present of* بودن to be.

It is unnecessary to multiply examples, but it will save the learner much trouble if he keep in mind, that the principal of those prefixed particles are,

ال *the Arabic particle* the.

ب (*or* بي *before words beginning with* ا) *the characteristic of the first future, and sometimes of the imperative.*

به *or* ب *the preposition* to, for, &c.

ب *prefixed sometimes by way of pleonasm, to which no translation can give any precise meaning.*

با with.

بي without.

ز *(for* از) from, with, by, &c.

كِ *(for* كه) which, what.

م مي *or* همي *characteristics of the present tense.— These characteristics of the present are frequently omitted by the Persian authors.*

م (*or* مي *before words beginning with* ا) *the negative prefixed to imperatives.*

نه or ن (or ني before words beginning with ا*) the general negative prefixed to all other tenses.**

The particles which are commonly annexed to words are as follow:

The possessive pronouns

ام م *or* يم my, mine.	ما our.
ات ت *or* يت thy, thine.	شما your.
و his, her, its.	ش *or* يش their.

ان *the plural of nouns having reference to living creatures.*

ها *the plural of inanimate nouns.*

ا *or* يا *the poetic vocative.*

را *the termination of the oblique cases.*

ست *the third person present of* بودن to be.

ي *is sometimes equivalent to our* a *or* one; *and at other times after nouns ending with* ا *or* ه *it marks that the following noun is in the genitive case; and it is then equal to our* of.

* *Notwithstanding the above observations, which will save the learner some perplexity in consulting dictionaries, many of the compounded words, and such oblique tenses as differ most from their infinitives, are for his greater ease and satisfaction inserted in this Index.*

The Persian writers make frequent use of the contracted infinitive; when the learner therefore cannot find such words as پرسید *or* ترسید *in the Index, let him look for* پرسیدن ترسیدن &c.

*** *The* A *put after some words in the Index shows that they are of Arabic original.*

INDEX.

ا ح

آب Water, fountain : lustre.

ابر upon : a cloud.

ابرار A *pl. of* برّ the just.

آبرنگ colour, paint, *comp. of* آب water *and* رنگ, colour.

ابسال A. Absāl, *proper name*.

ابوفضل A. Abūfażal (father of virtue) *proper name*.

ابوليث A. Abūlays (father of the lion) *proper name*

ات (*annexed to words*) thy.

آتش fire. آتشين fiery.

اثر A. a mark, impression.

اجستن to plant.

احداق A. *pl. of.* حدقة the eyes.

احرار A. *pl. of* حرّ the noble, free.

احزين A. *or.* احزان care, grief.

احسان A. a present, favour, benefit.

احمد A. Ahmad (most worthy of praise) *a proper name*.

احوال A. *pl. of* حل affairs, conditions; secrets.

آختن to draw *a sword, knife, &c*.

اختيار A. choice, liberty; prudence.

آخر A. end, finally; another.

آخرين A. moderns; posterity.

ادم A. Adam; a man: a messenger.

اذا A. when.

اذار the 9th Persian month; vernal.

آذر fire.

آذربجان the province of Media

آر bringing, bring thou, *from* آوردن

آزاي *or* آرا adorning, *from*

آراستن to adorn.

آرام rest.

ارزد is worth, *from* ارزیدن

آرد may bring, *from* آوردن

ارشاد A. safety, rectitude.

ارم Iram, *name of a fabulous garden in the East.*

از from.

آزاد کرد he set at liberty.

آزادي liberty.

آزار afflicting, *from*

آزاردن to rebuke, afflict, wound.

از آن from that.

از آنجا thence,

از این from this.

از اینجا hence.

از بهر on account of.

از بهرچه wherefore? why?

از جهت on account of.

آزرده afflicted, *from* آزردن

ازکجا whence. .

آزما experienced, *from* آزمودن

آزمایش temptation, experience.

آزمودن to try, tempt.

ازمیان from amidst.

ازیکدیگر from one another.

اژدن to sew together.

آسا like, resembling: appeasing.

آسایش rest, *both from* اسودن

اسب or اسپ a horse.

استماع A. hearing, sound.

استماع نمودندي they listened.

اسرار A. *pl. of* سرّ secrets.

اسمان heaven.

آسودن to rest.

اش (*annexed to words*) his

اشک a tear.

آشکار clear, evident.

آشناي love, friendship, familiarity: knowledge.

آشوب disturbing, *from*

آشوفتن to disturb.

آشیانه a nest.

اضطراب A. confusion, pain.

اطراف A. *pl. of* طرف parts, tracts.

اعتدال A. equality, temperance.

اعتقاد A. belief, faith.

اعظم A. great; greater.

اغاز a beginning.

اغصان A. *pl. of* اغصن branches.

اغوشتن to embrace.

اغیار A. *pl. of* غیر rivals, jealousy.

اغیشتن to cut.

آفتاب the sun.

آفتابه or آبتابه a bottle; a coffer.

افتادن to fall.

افراز exalting, *from* افراختن

افراسیاب Afrāṣiyāb, *proper name.*

افروختن to inflame.

افروز inflaming, *from the above.*

افریدن to create.

افرین creating, *from the above*

افزا or افزاي increasing, *from*

افزودن to increase.

افزون increasing.

افسوس alas!

افشاردن to speak idly.

افشان sprinkling, shedding.

افشاندن to sprinkle, shed.

افشردن to press.

افگن throwing, *from*

افگندن to throw.

اقداح A. *pl. of* قدح cups.

اقداحهم A. their cups.

اقرار A. affirmation, confirmation

اکبر A. Akbar (greater) *proper name.*

اگه *or* داه ' intelligent, vigilant knowledge.

اگر if. ا درچه though.

آ دن filling. اگندن to fill.

اکنون now.

آگین full.

ال A. *the article* the.

الا A. but, except.

التفات A. esteem, respect.

التیام A. gentleness, lenity.

الحان A. musical notes.

الضمیر A. the mind.

الف A. a thousand.

الود sprinkled, stained, *from*

الودن to stain, sprinkle.

الهي A. O God, heaven; divine.

اليد A. *the Arab. article prefixed to* يد aid, strength, hand, &c.

ام (*annexed to words*) my.

آمادن to prepare; to be ready.

آماز preparing.

امان A. security, mercy; sincerity.

آمد he came; coming.

آمدن to come, approach: the coming, approach.

آمدوشد coming and going.

امروز to-day.

امشب to-night.

آموختن to learn, teach.

آموز skilled, teaching.

آميختن to mix.

اميد hope. اميدوار hopeful.

امير a prince, noble.

اميرخواند شاه Amīrkh'āndshāh, *proper name.*

آميز mixing, *from* آميختن

آن that: time: now.

انان those.

انباشتن to fill.

انتظار A. desire, expectation.

آنجا there, in that place.

انجم A. or انجام stars.

انداختن to throw, dart.

انداز throwing, *from the above.*

اندرون within.

اندک little.

اندوختن to gain, gather.

اندودن to besmear.

اندوز gathering, gaining.

انديش thought, consideration.

آنسو thither.

آنکه that which; he who.

آنگه *or* انگاه then, at that time.

انگاشتن to think.

انگيختن to excite, raise.

انگيز raising, exciting.

انوار A. Anwār (splendour). *proper name.*

انها those.

انهار A. *pl. of* نهر rivers.

اوي or او or و he, she, it: his, her, its.

او خود himself, herself.

آواز a voice, sound: fame.

آوان A. *pl. of*. آن times.

اوبار devouring, swallowing, *from* اوباشتن to devour.

آور bringing, *from* آوردن

اورا him, her, it; to him, &c.

اوراق A. *pl. of* ورق leaves.

آوردن to bring.

اورنگ a throne: a manufacturing village.

اوضاع A. *pl. of* وضع affairs, actions.

اوّل A. first: the beginning.

اوّلين A. forefathers, the ancients.

اويختن to hang.

اهل A. skilful: endowed with, possessed of: people.

اهل حكمت wise.

اهو a fawn.

اي coming; come thou, *from* آمدن

اي or ايا O! *sign of the voc. case.*

ايام A. times, days, *pl. of* يوم

ايستادن to stand.

ايشان they; their. ايشان خود themselves. ايشانرا them: to them.

اي عزيز O Sir!

ايمن A. the right hand.

اين this. اينان these.

اينجا here.

اينچنين so, thus.

اينسو hither.

اينک behold.

آينه a mirror.

اينها these.

آيين nature.

ب

ب with; to, for.

با with, possessed of: since.

باب A. a gate; a chapter.

بابر Bābar, *a proper name.*

باختن to play.

باد the wind, air; let it be.

باد صبا zephyr; a gentle gale, the east *or* morning wind.

باده wine.

بار a load, baggage.

پارسي Persian.

باري once.

باز playing, play thou, *from* باختن

باز again, anew.

بازداشتن with-hold, keep back.

بازنده a player: playing.

باش being, be thou, *from* بودن

باشا a bāshā, governor.

باشد it may be; it may happen. *from* بودن

پاشيدن to sprinkle, diffuse.

باغ a garden. باغبان a gardener.

بافتن to weave: to tinge.

باقي A. the remainder; permanent.

باك fear, care.

پاك pure, chaste, clean.

پاكباز affectionate.

پاكتر more pure.

پاكدامن innocent, unblemished.

پاكرو beautiful, amiable.

پاكيزه gentle, pure, lovely.

بال a wing: an arm.

بالا above, upwards.

پالودن to strain.

بامداد in the morning.

پانزده fifteen.

پانصد five hundred.

باهم together.

بايد it is necessary, *from* بايستن

پايدار permanent, *from* پاي a foot, *and* دار *the participle of* داشتن to have.

بايستن to be necessary.

پايستن to accept.

ببرد he took *or* bore up.

بترس fear thou, *from* ترسيدن

ببوسيد he kissed, *from* بوسيدن *The first* ب *appears to be redundant.*

بچه (*pl.* بچگان) an infant.

بجهت for.

بحر A. metre: the sea.

بحررجز A. the Iambic measure.

بحررمل A. the Trochaic measure.

بحرهزج A. a kind of verse, consisting of Iambics and Spondees.

بحرين A *dual of* بحر the two seas.

بخارا Bokhārā, *name of a place.*

پختن to boil.

بخشم I would give, *from*

بخشيدن to give.

بد bad. بدم bad of me.

بدآن to *or* for these.

بدان know thou. بدانستمي I might have known, *from* دانستن

بده give thou, *from* دادن

پديد conspicuously, publicly.

پديدآمدن to become conspicuous.

پذير accepting, *from*

پذيرفتن to accept.

پر full. بر the bosom: upon.

برت upon thy bosom. بر carrying, ravishing, *from* بردن

براسودن to rest.

براسودمي I should rest.

برآمدن to ascend.

براي for, because.

برايد arises, comes, *from* برآمدن

بربط a harp, lute.

پرتو a ray, splendour.

برخاستن to rise, arise.

پرداختن to finish, compose.

پرداز composing, completing.

پردازد he finishes, performs.

پرداشتن to raise, exalt.

بردن to bear, carry, lead.

بردند they carried off.

پرده a veil, tapestry.

پردهداري a chamberlain, porter.

پرس ask thou, asking.

برسد it arrives.

برسر above, on the top *or* head.

پرسيدن to ask.

پرسیده ایم we have asked.

برفت he went away.

برگ a leaf; power; arms; ornament: a musical instrument.

پرکردن to fill.

برگشتن to return, recede.

برنشستن to ascend, mount.

پروانه a butterfly, moth.

پرور a protector, nourisher; educating; educate thou.

پروردن to educate, nourish.

پرورش education. Nourishment.

برون without, out of.

برهم together.

برهیختن to beware, abstain.

پرهیز abstinence, chastity.

پري an angel, fairy.

پریشان ruinous, disordered, scattered.

بزیر under, below.

پژمردن to wither, decay.

بسپارند they will give up, *from* سپردن

بستان a garden: پستان a breast.

بستن to bind, shut.

پسر a boy, child.

بسیار much, many.

بشگفتي it blossomed.

بشکنیم let us break.

بصیرت A. sight. prudence.

بطال A. lazy; a miscreant.

بطل A. vain, fruitless.

بعد after, بعد ازآن afterwards.

بفرما *second person imperative, from* فرمودن to command, &c.

بکامست is to my desire.

بکاوید he shall dig, *from* کافتن

بگذار leave thou.

بگو say thou, *from* گفتن.

بگذرد it shall pass, *from* گذردن

بل but.

بلا A. misfortune; without.

بلاد A. a country, region.

بلبل a nightingale.

بلكه but.

پلنگ a tiger.

بلي A. yes.

بميرد it shall perish, *from* مردن

بنابرين therefore.

بنال mourn thou, *from* ناليدن

پنج five. پنجاه fifty.

پنجم the fifth.

بند binding, compiling; bind thou.

پند advice, counsel.

پنداشتن to suppose, think.

بندد can bind, *from* بستن

بنفشه‌زار a garden of violets.

بنمود showed, *from* نمودن: *the* ب *prefixed seems to be redundant.*

بودن to be.

بودندي they were, *from* بودن

پوده a little branch.

پوزش an excuse.

بوس a kiss.

بوستان a garden.

بوسيد he kissed, *from* بوسيدن

پوشيدن to hide, cover, conceal.

بوم an owl. ببوم to the owl.

بوي fragrance, smell.

بوي گل rose-scented. Scent of the rose.

به good: in, into. To.

بهار the spring.

بهارستان the mansion of the spring.

بهجت cheerfulness.

بهر because, for, on account of: all, every one: fortune; pre-excellence.

بهرام Baharām (the planet Mars) *proper name.*

پهلوي the breast, side: near: the ancient Persian language.

بهم together, one with another.

بي without.

بيا come thou, *from* آمدن

بيابان a desart: uncultivated.

بيابم I shall find.

بيار bring thou, *from* آوردن

بياض A. white; brightness.

پياله a cup.

بيباک fearless.

بيامان faithless, merciless.

بياموزي thou shalt learn, *from* آموختن

بيت A. house; a distich.

بيتامّل inconsiderate.

بيترتيت irregular.

بيحواله without assistance.

بيخ a root, origin.

بيخار without a thorn.

بيخبر ignorant.

بيختن to sift.

پيختن to take captive.

بيحقيقت false, faithless.

پيدا openly: a discovery.

بيدل heartless, disconsolate.

پير old; an old man.

پيرا adorning, collecting.

پيراستن to deck.

بيرون without, out of doors.

بيز shedding, sifting, *from* بيختن

بيست twenty.

پيش before; the front.

بيشمار innumerable.

بيقرار inconstant; afflicted.

بيگانه new. بيگانگي novelty.

پيکر the face, form.

پيل an elephant.

بيم fear, danger.

بيمثال unequalled.

پيمودن to measure.

بين seeing.

بينم I may see, *both from* ديدن

بي انتها *or* بينتها endless.

بينوا helpless, unfortunate.

پيوستن to join, touch.

پيوند touching, joining, reaching.

ت

ات *or* ت *(annexed to words)* thy.

تا until, that, in order to.

تاب heat, flame; splendour; strength; desire; a fever; contorsion.

تابانيدن to cause to shine.

تابم I may turn, &c. *from*

تابيدن to turn, twist; to shine, make warm; to be able.

تابناک bright, shining.

تاختن to twist; hasten; wager.

تار obscurity; a hair; a wire; a thread; the summit.

تاراج spoil, prey, ruin.

تاري obscurity, darkness.

تاريخ A. a history, chronicle.

تاريک dark. تاريکتر darker.

تازه fresh, new, young.

تازهتر more fresh, &c.

تافتن to inflame, burn.

تامل A. consideration, speculation.

تبا let alone, leave, relinquish.

تحفه A. a present; rare, elegant.

تدبير A. prudence, advice; government; regulation.

تذکره A. a record, obligation.

تر moist, fresh.

ترا thee; to the.

ترانه harmony, modulation.

تربت A. a tomb.

ترتيب A. order, regularity.

ترسي thou fearest, *from*

ترسيدن to fear.

ترسيدي thou mayst fear.

تشوير A. pointing; shame, anguish.

ترک A. a beautiful man *or* woman; a Turk; leaving, relinquishing.

تصحيح correcting; arranging.

تصنيف A. composition, invention.

تعالي الاه A. *or* الاه تعالي omnipotent God.

تعجيل A. haste.

تعليق A. hanging, dependant; the most elegant kind of Persian hand-writing.

تغافل A. negligence: contempt.

تفرج A. relaxation, walking; contemplation.

تلخ bitter; severely.

تلخکام bitter in the mouth.

تماشا diversion; a spectacle, seeing.

تمام A. full, perfect; completion, end: completely.

تمنا A. a wish; supplication.

تن the body, person.

تنها alone, only; solitary.

تو thou: thy. تو خود thyself.

تواريخ A. (*pl. of* تاريخ) histories.

توان it is possible, *from* توانستن

توبه A. repentance; conversion.

توختن to collect; to pay debts.

تهنيت A. congratulation.

تهي wretched, empty, naked, poor.

تير an arrow: the river Tigris.

تيز sharp; violent, passionate.

تيغ a sword.

ث

ثري A. moisture.

ثريا A. the constellation Pleïades.

ثمين A. precious: the eighth.

ج

جا a place.

جادو an inchanter; inchanting.

چاره a remedy.

چاک a fissure, a breach.

چاک زدن to tear.

جام a cup, glass; mirror.

جامه a mantle, robe; bed.

جامي a collection.

جان the soul; a beautiful woman.

جانان souls, friends; lovers.

جان فزاي delighting the soul

جانور having life, an animal.

جبين A. the forehead.

جدّ A. study, endeavour.

چرا wherefore, why?

جراحت (*pl.* جراحات) a wound.

چرخ fortune; the world, globe.

چرکس Circassia.

جريمه A. a crime.

جزا *or* جز except, unless.

جستن to leap; to seek, examine.

چشم an eye.

چشمه a fountain.

چشیدن to taste, try.

چشیده‌ام I have tasted.

جعد A. a curling lock.

چغانه a kind of musical instrument, a lyre, a lute.

جگر the liver, جگردوز liver-piercing.

چکني what dost thou do? *comp. of* چ (for چه) what, *and the second person pres. of* کردن

چگونه how? what?

جلال‌الدین Jalāluddīn (the glory of religion) *proper name.*

جلد A. a volume: a skin.

جمال A. beauty, elegance.

جمشید Jamshēd, *proper name.*

جمع A. collection, assembly, troops.

چمن a garden, meadow.

چمنزار a verdant plain, meadow.

چنان in like manner.

چنانچه in the same way.

چنانکه in this manner, thus.

جنّت A. *or* جنه paradise.

چند how many?

چند بار how often?

جنستان fairy land.

چنگ a harp, lute.

چو when (*or* چنین) like, as.

جو seek thou, *from* جستن

جواب an answer.

جوان young, a young man.

جواني youth.

جواهر A. (*pl. of* جوهر) jewels.

چون how? when.

چونکه when that.

جویني Jawīnī, *name of an author.*

جویي thou mayst seek, *from* جستن

چه what, which.

جه leaping, *from* جستن

چهار four.

چهارده fourteen.

چهارصد four hundred.

چهارم the fourth.

جهان the world.

جهانگشا conqueror of the world

جهاندار possessing the world.

جهد A. diligence, solicitude.

چهل forty.

چي what? چيست what is it?

چيد he gathered, *from* چيدن

چه ميجوي what dost thou seek?

چه ميگوي what dost thou say?

چين China: a ringlet.

چينم I may gather, *from* چيدن

ح

حاجت A. necessity: poverty.

حاصل A. arriving; completion; harvest, produce: profit.

حافظ A. Hāfiẓ (a man of great memory) *name of a poet.*

حال A. a condition, state: a thing: time present.

حالت motion, action; state.

حبس A. imprisonment.

حدايق A. (*pl. of* حديقه) gardens.

حديث A. news; an accident.

حذر A. caution.

حركت A. motion: a vowel.

حسد A. envy, malevolence.

حسن A. beauty, elegance.

حشمت A. followers, troops.

حقّ A. true: truth, reason.

حقيقت A. sincerity: truly.

حكم A. a decree; wisdom.

حكمت A. science; a miracle.

حكيم A. wise; a doctor, learned man, philosopher, physician.

حلال A: lawful

حمّام A. a bath.

حمد A. praise.

حوادث A. *pl. of* حادث) accidents, news.

حواله A. assistance, support: a fortress; eminence, mountain.

حوايج A. (*pl of* حاجت) necessaries, necessities: things.

حيات A. life; a portico, vestibule.

حيل A. (*pl. of* حيلة) frauds.

حيوان A. living, life; an animal.

خ

خار a thorn.

خارخار anguish, resentment.

خاستن to rise.

خاصّ A. pure, excellent; noble.

خاطر A. mind, heart, disposition.

خاقاني Khākānī, *name of a poet.*

خاك earth, dust.

خال A. a mole *on the face.*

خالق A. the Creator.

خان a lord, grandee; an inn.

خانها (*pl. of* خانه) houses.

خبر A. history; news; fame.

خبرده relate thou, *from*

خبردادن to inform, relate.

ختن Khotan, *Tartary.*

خجل A. ashamed, blushing; envy.

خجلت A. a blush, shame.

خدا God.

خداوند a prince, lord, patron.

خداوندا O God! O heaven!

خداوند يكانه the only Lord God.

خدايار friend of God, *proper name.*

خرامان stately, pompous.

خرّت A. murmured: fell, *from* خرّ

خرد intellect: small.

خرده minute, subtile; minutiæ.

خرسند contented. خرسندم I am contented. خرسندي content.

خرم charming, pleasant.

خروس a cock *or* hen.

خروش rage, emotion: an attack.

خريد buying; he bought.

خزان the autumn.

خسرو Khosrū, *Cyrus.*

خضر A. Khiżar, *proper name.*

خطّ A. a mustacho; a line, rule.

خطا A. a crime, error.

خفقان palpitation of the heart.

خلاصت A. the best part of any thing, the substance, cream.

خلوص A. sincerity, purity.

خندان smiling, pleasant.

خواب sleep; a dream.

خواب الود drowned in sleep.

خوابَجا the place of rest; a bed.

خوارا eating, devouring.

خواستن to be willing; to want.

خوان a reader, singer, singing: viands, victuals; a table.

خواندن to read, sing.

خواه ask, call, wish for.

خواهي you will, *from* خواستن

خوب pleasant, fair, gentle, good.

خوبتر more beautiful, &c.

خوبترين most beautiful.

خوب روي fair-faced.

خود *or* خودش one's self; his.

خوردن to eat, devour.

خورشيد the sun.

خوش sweet; happy.

خوشا joy be to—

خوشبوي sweet-scented.

خوشخوي sweet-tempered.

خون blood. خونريز blood-dropping.

خوي disposition, temper.

خويدن to chew the cud.

خيال imagination, phantasy; a spectre: vain, fruitless.

خيز rising, *from* خاستن *or*

خيزيدن to rise, spring up.

خيزيدي thou hast risen.

د

داج darkness, night.

داد equity; a gift; lamentation.

دادن to give.

دار having, *from* داشتن

دار A. a family; house; town.

دارا Dārā, *Darius*.

دارم I have, enjoy, possess.

دارند they have *or* hold.

داشت he had.

داشتن to have, hold.

داغ a wound, scar, mark.

دام a net, snare, trap.

دامن a fold, lappet, *or* hem, skirt, border of a garment.

دان knowing: a vessel; sheath.

دانا a wise *or* learned man.

دانايانه prudently, wisely.

دانستم I knew.

دانستن to knew.

دانش learning.

دانشمند learned; a doctor.

دانشمندي learning, literature.

دانند they know, *from* دانستن

دانه snare, allurement; a grain: cannon ball.

داني thou knowest, dost thou know?

داوري A. dominion, administration of justice.

در in, above; around: a gate.

درّ (*pl. of* دُرّة) A. pearls.

درامدن to enter.

دراوردن to carry in.

دراويختن to suspend; contend; provoke.

درخت a tree, a plant.

درخواستن to require, demand.

درد a wound, pain, torment: dregs.

درست right, complete.

درشت harsh, hard.

درگرو بود was betrothed.

درنگ delay.

درنگرد he beholds, *from*

درنگرستن to view, behold.

درون within: the heart; intrails.

دري the Persian language.

دريا the sea.

دريافتن to understand.

دريغا *or* دريغ alas!

دست the hand.

دشمن an enemy.

دفتر a register, journal; index.

دقيقت A. minute; subtile, small; a subtilty: a minute.

درگذر depart from, leave.

درگذشت it passes away.

دگر again: another.

دل the heart.

دلاويز ravishing, delightful, *comp. of* دل *and* اويز *participiple of* اويختن to exalt, suspend.

دلجو agreeable, salutary, *comp. of* دل *and* جو (*for* جوي) *part. of* جستن to desire, ask, seek.

دلدار as mistress; heart-ravishing, *comp. of* دل *and* دار *particip. of* داشتن to have, hold.

دلسوز heart-wounding, *comp. of* دل *and* سوز *part. of* سوختن to burn.

دلفريب heart-deceiving, *comp. of* دل *and* فريب *part. of* فريفتن to deceive.

دلكشي heart-conquering, *comp. of* دل *and* كشي *from* كشيدن to open, conquer, &c.

دم time: breath: pleasure.

دماغ the brain, the palate.

دمساز a friend; harmony, ***comp.*** *of* دم breath, and ساز *from* ساختن to do, make.

دو two.

دوحت A. a species of large trees; an orchard: rattles for children.

دور A. a circle, orbit, revolution: rolling. دور P. far off, distant.

دوري distance, absence.

دوز sewing, piercing.

دورده *for* دوازده twelve.

دوست a friend, mistress.

دوستر dearer, more friendly.

دوصد two hundred.

دولت *or* دوله A. felicity; riches; a kingdom, state.

دوم the second.

ده a village; a giver: ten.

دهر fortune, fate, time, world.

دهش a gift, liberality.

دهشت fear, astonishment.

دهقان a villager.

ده هزار ten thousand.

دي winter, first winter month, December; yesterday.

ديار (*pl. of* دار) friends, families. habitations: a country.

ديد he saw, *from*

ديدن to see.

ديدار sight.

ديروز yesterday.

ديگر another. ديگربار again.

ديوان a collection of an author's works, chiefly poetical: a royal court, tribunal of justice. A great officer of government sô called.

ذ

ذو A. possessed of, endowed with.

ذو جلال A. majestic.

ذهب gold.

ر

راحت A. tranquillity.

راز a secret, mystery.

راغ a declivity, foot of a hill.

رافت A. compassion, favour.

راندن to drive, banish.

راه a way, path.

راه زدن to rob, steal, infest the highway.

رايحه A. fragrant; fragrance.

رباعي A. a verse of four lines, a word of four letters.

رجوع A. returning.

رخ a cheek, face; a groan; the sound of a musical instrument.

رخسار a cheek.

رساله A. an embassy; a mandate.

رسانيدن to cause to arrive.

رستن to grow; to be delivered.

رسم A. manner, law, regulation.

رسيد arrives, *from*

رسيدن to arrive.

رشته a line, thread.

رشيد A. Rashīd (a conductor): *proper name*.

رعنا A. tender, delicate, lovely.

رفتار motion.

رفتم I went, *from*

رفتن to go: departure.

رقصیدن to dance: motion

رقم A. colouring, painting, embroidery: writing; a letter, character; arithmetic.

رکناباد Roknābād, *name of a place.*

رموز A. (*pl. of* رمز) enigmas.

رمي A. he threw; throwing.

رنج sorrow, pain.

رند a wanton, dissolute, drunken person.

رنگ colour paint.

رنگارنگ many-coloured, various.

رنگین coloured.

روا A. right, competent, worthy.

روح A. the soul, life, spirit.

روحافزا spirit-raising, *from* افزودن

رودکي Rūdakī, *proper name.*

روز a day.

روزافزون increasing daily.

روزگار fortune, world, time, an age; wind, air, vanity.

روزگار نامه a journal.

روزي one day: fortune.

روشن splendid, evident.

روشنتر more splendid.

روشني light, splendour.

روضت a garden.

رونق A. beauty, elegance.

روي *or* رو face, top, surface.

روي thou dost go, *from* رفتن

رويي thou dost grow, *from* رستن

ره a road, way.

ريحان A. herbs (*in general*) *properly* sweet basil.

ريختن to pour.

ريز pouring, dropping.

ريستن to buzz.

ز

ز (*for* از) from: if.

زادن to be born; to bring forth.

زار a complaint: a bed, a place.

زاريدن to complain.

ژاله dew; frost, hoar frost, hail.

زبان the tongue; language.

زبده A. the most excellent of any thing, the flour, cream.

زبر above, high, superiour.

زخم a wound, blow, stroke.

زدا dispelling.

زدن to strike, hurt, impel.

زدودن to polish.

زر gold.

زرد pale, yellow.

زرگر a goldsmith.

زرنگار ornamented with gold.

زرين golden.

زستن to live.

زکه from whom?

زلف a lock of hair.

زليخا Zulaykhā, *Potiphar's wife.*

زمان A. the world; fortune; time, season.

زمردفام emerald-coloured.

زمردين made of emeralds.

زمين ground, earth.

زن striking, disturbing, *from* زدن to strike. A woman.

زندان a prison.

زندگاني life.

زوال A. decay, misery.

زهر poison, venom.

زهرناک poisonous.

زهره Venus; courage; gall.

زيان loss damage.

زيب an ornament; beauty.

زيبا beautiful.

زيباتر more beautiful.

زيبد agrees, *from.*

زيبيدن to quadrate, agree with.

زير under, below.

زيرا because, for.

س

سا like, resembling.

ساحل A. a shore, coast, bank.

ساختن to prepare, make.

سار full of.

ساز preparing.

سازد he makes, *both from* ساختن

سازنده a composer, performer.

ساغر a cup.

ساق A. the leg.

ساقي A. a cup-bearer, water-carrier.

سالك A. a traveller; going.

ساله a year, age.

سايه a shade.

سبب A. a cause, motive.

سپردن to resign, commit, give in charge; recommend, charge, enjoin.

سبك light of weight.

سبكباران bearers of light burdens.

سپوختن to prick.

سپه a soldier, soldiery, army.

سپيده white.

سپيده دام the morning, aurora.

ستاشتن to take, ravish.

ستان taking; a country.

ستايش praise, *from* ستودن

ستدن to take.

ستردن to shave, erase, efface.

ستم injury, oppression, tyranny. threatening.

ستمديدگان the injured, afflicted.

ستمگار a tyrant.

ستمگر the wicked.

ستمكيش a tyrant.

ستودن to praise.

سجاده A. a kind of carpet.

سجع A. rhyme, melody; the cooing of doves.

سجود A. adoration.

سجيت A. disposition, temper.

سحر A. the morning, crepuscule; inchantment.

سحرگاه *or* سحرگه the morning.

سحري A. belonging to the morning.

سختي adversity, danger, poverty.

سخن speech; a word.

سر head, end, extremity; love, desire: principal, supreme.

سراج A. a lamp, lantern; the sun.

سراسر from beginning to end.

سرافراز lofty, tall; glorious.

سردادن to banish to a place, to confine.

سرشتن to mix, compose.

سرگذشت an occurrence, accident: a tale, song, warbling.

سرگشته wanton; astonished, confused: a vagabond.

سرو a cypress-tree; a horn.

سرور A. joy: a prince, chief.

سریش mixing, *from* سرشتن

سزا convenient, proper.

سزاي it is proper.

سعادتمند of a good disposition: happy, august.

سعدي Saʿdī, *name of a poet.*

سعي A. an endeavour, diligence.

سفتي thou piercest, *from*

سفتن to pierce, bore.

سکندر Sakandar, *Alexander.*

سکون A. quiet, resignation.

سلسال A. pure water: a chain.

سلسله A. a chain, series, lineage.

سلمان A. Salmān, *proper name.*

سليم A. Salīm (perfect, unblemished) *proper name.*

سمرقندي a native of Samarkand.

سمن jessamine.

سمنبر jessamine-bosomed.

سنبل a hyacinth.

سنبلستان a garden of hyacinths.

سنگ a stone.

سنگين stony.

سواد A. blackness; melancholy.

سوختن to burn, inflame.

سودمي I would touch, rub, *from*

سودن to stroke, rub, touch.

سوري a beautiful kind of red rose.

سوز inflaming, *from* سوختن

سوگند an oath.

سوي towards; a place, part, side.

سه three.

سها Sohā, *name of a star.*

سهي tall, erect.

سهيل *the star* Canopus; *name of a* Persian *author.*

سي thirty.

سياه *or* سيه black.

سياهي blackness.

سيراب bathed, full of water.

سيزده thirteen.

سيصد three hundred.

سيم silver.

سيما the face, colour.

سيمين silvered.

سينه the bosom, breast.

سيوم the third.

ش

اش *or* ش (*annexed to words*) his, her: to him, to her.

شاخ a branch, twig, horn.

شادماني mirth.

شام the evening.

شامگاه in the evening.

شان (*for* ايشان) they; their.

شاندن to comb.

شانزده sixteen.

شاه a king, emperor.

شاهوش royal, princely.

شب night.

شباب A. youth.

شبي one night.

شتاب haste.

شتابي *or* شتاب‌كن make haste.

شتافتن to make haste.

شتر (*pl.* شتران *or* شترها) a camel.

شجر A. a tree.

شجع A. strength, force, agility.

شد he was: going, *from* شدن to be, &c.

شراب wine.

شرمسار bashful.

شرمساري bashfulness.

شستن to wash.

شش six. شست sixty.

شعرا A. (*pl of* شاعر) poets, learned men, doctors.

شعله A. light, flame, splendour.

شکار a hunter.

شکاف breaking, *from*

شکافتن to cleave, tear break.

شکایت A. a complaint.

شکر sugar.

شکرخوارا eating sugar.

شکردن to hunt, take, seize.

شکردان
شکرستان } a chest of sugar.

شکرلب sugar-lipped.

شکستن to break, defeat.

شکسته Shikastah (broken) *the current Persian hand-writing.*

شگفتن to blossom; to admire.

شگند they blossom, *from the above.*

شگوفه a flower.

شکیبا patient.

شکیبایي patience, toleration.

شما you, your. شما خود your-selves.

شمار number; numerous.

شمارا ye, you; to you.

شمامه A. odour, fragrance.

شمردن to number, enumerate.

شمس A. the sun; gold.

سمشیر a scymitar.

شمع A. a candle, wax taper.

شمه A. odour: nature, custom; an atom.

شناختن to understand.

شناس knowing, *from the above.*

شنفتن *or* شنودن to hear.

شنوده ام I have heard.

شنیدند they heard, *from* شنیدن

شوخ jovial, gay, wanton, bold, insolent.

شهد A. honey, honey-comb.

شهر A. a city; the moon; a knave.

شیدا insane; enamoured.

شیر a lion; also a tiger.

شیرازه the top band of a book.

شیرازي Shīrāzī, a native of Shīrāz.

شیرستان the habitation of lions.

شیرماده a lioness.

شیرنر a lion.

شیرین Shīrīn (sweet, gentle) *proper name.*

شیرینگار of gentle manners.

ص

صاحب A. a lord, master, possessor, friend: endowed with.

صاحب جمال beautiful.

صاحب‌دل honest-hearted.

صبا A. the zephyr; youth.

صبح *or* صباح A. morning, aurora.

صبحدم in the morning.

صبحدمی one morning.

صبر A. patience.

صبی A. a boy.

صحبت company, society.

صحیفه A. a leaf, book, page.

صد a hundred.

صددر Sad-dar (a hundred gates) *name of a* Persian *book.*

صد هزار a hundred thousand.

صرف کردن to expend, employ.

صعب A. difficult, severe.

صف a rank, file; order.

صفا A. purity, pleasure.

صمّا A. a calamity.

صوت A. voice, sound, noise.

صورت A. fancy, image, form; a spectre.

صورت کردن to feign.

صیام A. fasting; the season of fasting among the Mahomedans; *metaphorically* the spring.

صید A. hunting; prey.

صید کردن to take prisoner.

ض

ضمیر A. mind, conscience.

ضیا A. light, splendour.

ط

طرب A. joy, mirth, festivity.

طربخانه the house of mirth.

طرف A. a border, margin, part.

طرّه A. a lock of hair.

طریق A. custom, way, manner.

طلبي thou askest, *from* طلبيدن

طلوع A. rising, *as the sun.*

طمع A. desire, avarice.

طواب A. a circuit, walk.

طوطي a parrot.

طوفان the deluge. A storm.

طي A. a fold, ply: folding.

طير A. a bird.

ظ

ظفر A. victory.

ظلمت A. darkness.

ع

عادت A. custom, usage.

عارض A. a cheek; a tooth; an accident; a heavy cloud.

عاشق A. a lover.

عاشقين A. two lovers.

عاقبه A. the end, issue, event, success; finally.

عالم A. the world, time; learned.

عالم سوزي enlightener, *or* inflamer of the world.

عام A. universal: plebeian, public.

عباسي A. ɛabbāṣī, *name of a dynasty of Arabian khalifs.*

عبادنگاه a place of worship.

عبرت A. wonder, mystery, example.

عجب A. wonder, admiration.

عدالت A. justice.

عدو A. an enemy.

عذار A. a cheek, face, temples.

عراب A. a wild Arab.

عرب A. an Arabian inhabiting a city.

عرصه A. a field, court, area; an empty space: a dice-table.

عروض A. poetry, prosody.

عزيز A. magnificent, incomparable.

عشرت A. mirth, conversation; the pleasures of the table.

عشق A. love.

عشق بازي fondness.

عصمت A. chastity, integrity; defence, safeguard.

عطر A. perfume, ottar of roses.

عطرسا perfumed, fragrant.

عفاق الله A. God preserve.

عقد A. a string of pearls: a knot; a treaty.

عقل A. prudence, memory, art, knowledge; a narrative.

عقوبت A. punishment, torment.

علم A. knowledge, science, art.

علما A. (*pl. of* عليم) learned men.

عمر A. life. عمرم my life.

عمل A. action, operation.

عنبر A. amber, ambergris.

عندليب A. a nightingale.

عنكبوت A. a spider.

عوايب A. (*pl. of* عيب) vices.

عهد A. age, time; compact, promise.

عيار A. a touchstone, proof.

عيب A. a vice, crime, stain.

عيد A. a festival, solemnity; joy.

عيش A. mirth, delight; life.

عين A. a fountain; an eye, look; gold; essence: paradise.

غ

غايب A. absent, invisible, concealed.

غبار A. dust; a thick vapour.

غريب A. a stranger, foreigner; extraordinary. A poor man.

غزال A. a fawn.

غزل A. an ode.

غزليات A. (*pl. of the above*) odes.

غصّه A. vexation. Anger.

غلام A. a boy, servant, slave.

غم A. care, grief, terror.

غمگين sorrowful.

غمناك afflicted.

غنچه a rose-bud. A bud.

غنودن to sleep, slumber.

ف

فاضت A. overflowed, *from* فيض

فال A. an omen, presage.

فام coloured.

فتنه A. a tumult, faction, discord, mischief, scandal.

فخر A. glorious; glory, ornament.

فدا A, ransom, redemption.

فراق A. absence, separation.

فراموش oblivion, *from*

فراموشیدن to forget.

فرّخ A. happy.

فردا to-morrow.

فردوسي Fardōṣī (belonging to paradise) *name of a poet.*

فرستادن to send.

فرشته an angel, messenger; fairy.

فرقت A. absence; a troop; a sect.

فرمودن to command.

فرو below; dejected.

فروخت selling: he sold, *from*

فروختن to sell.

فرود آمدن to descend.

فروزي (*for* افروزي) inflamed, *from* افروختن

فروش he sells, *both from* فروختن

فروغ A. splendour.

فروماندن to be dejected.

فريبي *or* فريب deceit, *from* فريفتن

فريدون Farīdūn, *name of a king.*

فريفتن to deceive.

فسردن to freeze, congeal.

فشان scattering, *from* فشاندن

فشردن to press, squeeze.

فصاحت A. eloquence, melody.

فغان sorrow, complaint: alas!

فكر A. consideration, care.

فكر بفرما consider; بفرما *is the imperative of* فرمودن

فگن throwing, throw thou, *from*

فگندن to throw, throw away, lay aside.

فلك A. heaven; the world; fortune.

في A. in, into.

فيض A. abundance: he diffused.

فيل an elephant.

ق

قاف Kāf, *the name of a fabulous mountain.*

قد A. a form, figure, shape, stature.

قدح A. a cup, goblet.

قدر A. fate, predestination; quantity; value; dignity, power.

قرار A. constancy, consistency, confirmation; quiet.

قرين A. contiguous, related to.

قصايد (pl. *of* قصيده) poems, elegies.

قصر A. a palace.

قصه A. a tale; an action.

قصيده A. an elegy, poem.

قضا A. fate, death, judgment; jurisdiction.

قطعه A. a fragment: segment, part.

قفس a cage.

قلعة A. (*pl.* قلعجات) a castle.

قلم A. a pen.

قلمگار a writer, an engraver.

قلوب (*pl. of* قلب) hearts.

قمر A. the moon.

قمروش like the moon.

قول A. a word, speech, eloquence.

قهر A. violence, force, oppression; power; chastisement; anger.

قياس A. measure; reasoning, thought, advice, argument; a syllogism.

قيام A. station, standing; resurrection; confusion, tumult.

قيصر A. Cesar, an emperor.

ك

ك A. as, like, in the same manner.

کاتبي A. Kātibī (a writer, secretary) *proper name.*

کاحداقي A. like my eyes, *comp. of* ک like, احداق eyes, *and* ي *the inseparable pronoun* my.

کادن to caress.

کار business, object; a maker.

کارخانه a work-shop, place of business; the world.

کارزار a battle, contest.

کارگر expert: one who labours, adjusts, penetrates, brings a thing to bear. Effective. Workmen.

کارگر آمدن to penetrate, labour, &c.

کاروان a caravan.

کاستن to lessen.

کاش would!

کاشانه a house, hall, gallery, chamber.

کافتن to dig.

کاکل a curling lock.

کالبد the body; a form, model.

کام desire, wish.

کامران desire; the obtaining one's wish.

گاه a place. کاه a straw: lessening.

کبر A. pride, magnificence.

کبوتر a dove.

کتاب A. a book, letter, writing.

کجا where? whither? how?

گداختن to melt, dispel.

گداز melting, *from the above.*

کدام who? کدامست who is there?

گذاشتن to leave, neglect.

گذرانیدن to pass through.

گذشتن to pass: to leave.

گر if: a performer, maker.

کرا whom; to whom? hire, rent.

گرازنده sporting, skipping, strutting.

گرچه though.

کرد business, labour: he made.

گردابي a whirlpool, gulf, precipice.

کردار action, labour, profession; life.

گردش جام the circling of the glass.

کردم I made, *from*

کردن to do, make.

گردن the neck.

گرز a battle-axe, mace.

گرفتن to take.

گرگ a wolf.

گرم warm. گرما warmth.

کرمان Carmania, *name of a place.*

گرو marriage, nuptials, betrothing, a pledge.

گري *or* گريه lamentation, weeping.

گريختن to flee, escape.

گريستن to weep.

کز that, which.

گزاردن to perform.

گزشتن to pass.

گزيدن to choose; to bite.

گزيده select, most excellent, noble, glorious: bitten.

کس a person, any one.

گستر spreading, strewing, *from*

گستردن to spread, strew, scatter.

گسيختن to break, tear.

گسيل breaking, *from the above.*

کشا conquering, opening, &c. *from*

کشادن to open, discover, conquer to rejoice.

کشايد he discovers, *from the above.*

گشتن to become: کشتن to kill.

گسستن to break, rend.

کشفتن to scatter, dissolve.

کشمير Kashmīr, *name of a place.*

کشود he has discovered, &c. *from*

کشودن to discover, open, conquer, delight.

کشور a region, climate, country.

کشيده ام I have suffered *or* drawn.

کف the hand, the palm.

گفت he said. گفتار speech.

گفتم I said.

گفتن to speak, say; speaking.

گفتي thou hast said; he said.

گُل (gul) a rose.

گِل (gil) clay.

گلاب rose-water.

کلاله hair, locks.

کلام a word, writing, oration.

گلاندام Gulandām (rose-resembling, *from* گل a rose, *and* اندام form, figure, &c.) *a proper name.*

کلاه a diadem, cap.

گلبن a rose-bush.

گلبوي rose-scented.

کلبه a closet, cottage, hut.

گلزار a bed of roses

گلستان Gulistān (a rose-garden, bower of roses) *title of a celebrated book.*

گلسوري a beautiful species of red rose.

گلشن a rose-garden.

گلعذار rose-cheeked.

گلفام rose-coloured.

گلفشان strewing flowers.

گلگشت a rose-walk; bower, delightful place.

گلگون rose-coloured.

کليات A. (*pl. of* کلي) the whole; universal. The whole works.

کم little; defective; absent.

گماشتن to insert, place, commit: to loose, liberate.

کمال A. perfection, accomplishment, finishing.

کمبها of little value.

کمتر less.

کمعقل with little sense.

کن do thou; doing, *from* کردن

کنار a boundary, margin, side, part, shore; an embrace.

گنبد a vault, arch, tower, cupola.

گند rotting, *from*

گنديدن *or* گندن to rot.

کنيز a servant maid, female slave.

کو where?

گو say thou, *from* گفتن

گوش an ear.

گوش‌کن listen thou, *from*

گوش‌کردن to listen.

گوشه a corner.

كوفتم I smote, *from*

كوفتن to smite.

گوناگون various, many-coloured.

كوه a mountain.

گوهر a jewel, pearl; lustre, essence; self-existing.

كه who, which: since.

كي who.

گيتي the universe.

گير taking.

گيرد might take, *both from* گرفتن

كيست who is it? *comp. of* كي who, است *third person present of* بودن

كينه *or* كين hatred, revenge, rancour. گين full of.

كين that these, *comp. of* ك *and* اين

ل

لاله a tulip.

لاله‌زار a border *or* bed of tulips.

لاندن to move.

لب (*pl.* لبان) a lip; margin.

لبّ A. the heart, pith, marrow.

لبالب up to the brim.

لشكر an army.

لشكركش a conquering army.

لطف A. benignity, gentleness, grace, favour, humanity, generosity.

لعل a ruby, ruby lip.

لك a lack, a hundred thousand.

للسجود A. for the worship (of God) *comp of* ل for, *and* ل *for the Arabic article* ال *and* سجود adoration.

لوليان A. the most precious sort of pearls; beautiful women.

ليث A. a lion.

ليكن but.

ليل A. Layl *or* ليله night.

ليلي Layla, *a woman's name.*

م

م (*annexed to words*) my.

ماء A. water, liquor, juice.

ما A. that, which.

ما we; our. ما خود ourselves.

ماده female: a woman.

مار a serpent.

مارا us; to us.

مالت A. bent, *from* ميل

ماليدن to rub, grind, polish.

ماندن to remain.

مانستن to resemble.

مانند they remain, from ماندن

ماه the moon: a month.

ماهرخ with cheeks like the moon.

ماهروي with a face like the moon.

ماهي lunar, monthly; a fish.

مايل A. inclining, having a propensity.

مبادا lest, by chance.

مبسوط A. extended, dilated, spread.

مپرس do not ask, *from* پرسيدن

مثال A. similitude, resemblance.

مثنوي A. rhyme.

مجلس A. an assembly, banquet.

مجنون A. Majnūn (distracted with love) *proper name.*

مجمع A. a place where people assemble; a collection, junction.

محبت A. love, friendship, benevolence; affection; company.

محبوب A. a friend; mistress; amiable, dear, beloved.

محبوس A. confined, imprisoned.

محرم A. a friend, counsellor; spouse, husband, wife; any one who from their station in a family is admitted into the *haram* or women's apartments.

محقر A. vile, contemptible, trifling.

محل A. place, time, opportunity.

محمد Muhammad (praise-worthy) *proper name.*

محنت A. affliction, disgrace.

مختصر A. contracted; an epitome.

مختلف A. discordant, confused.

مخزن a magazine, treasury.

مدبر A. governing; a governor, magistrate.

مدت A. a space of time.

مدهوش A. astonished, disturbed.

مذاق A. to taste; the taste, palate.

مرا me; to me.

مراحم A. (*pl. of* مرحمت) favours, graces.

مراد A. desire, will, affection.

مراهم A. (*pl. of* مرهم) remedies, plasters.

مرد *or* مردم a man, hero; brave.

مردانه courageously, manfully.

مردن to die; to be extinguished.

مروت A. courtesy, generosity.

مژده joyful tidings.

مست enamoured, intoxicated.

مستغني A. disdainful; rich; content.

مشام A. perfumed; the palate.

مشاهده A. the sight.

مشاهده نمودن to view.

مشرق A. the east.

مشغول A. attentive; attention.

مشک musk. مشکبوي smelling of musk. مشکين musky.

مصراع *or* ع A. an hemistich; one half of a folding door.

مصدر A. a source: infinitive.

مصلا Musalla, *name of a place.*

مضرت A. damage, disadvantage.

مطرب A. a singer, musician.

معذور A. an excuse.

معرکه A. a battle, field of battle.

معشوق A. a friend, beloved.

معشوقه A. a mistress.

معطّر A. scented, perfumed.

معقول A. reasonable, rational, probable, pertinent.

معما A. an enigma, mystery.

معني A. sense, idea, signification.

معهود A. established, known.

مغ A. a priest of the Parsees, Guebres *or* worshippers of fire.

مغبچگان cup-bearers.

مغز the brain, head, marrow, substance, *or* best part of any thing.

مفارقت A. separation, alienation.

مقام A. condition, station; dignity; office: residence: musical tone.

مقدار A. quantity, space, number.

مقصود A. intention, will, desire.

مقلب A. a conductor, mover, disposer.

مکافات A. a recompense, reward.

مگر perhaps, by chance; unless.

مل wine.

ملاح A. a sailor.

ملك A. a kingdom, power, possession, inheritance; an angel.

ملمعت A. rays of light.

من I: my. من خود myself.

منتها A. finished, concluded.

مند full of, endowed with.

منزل A. a house of entertainment, an inn; any place where travellers rest at night; a day's journey, a stage.

منصور A. a conqueror, triumpher.

منفعت A. advantages.

منقار A. a bird's bill.

منيار do not bring, *the imperat. of* آوردن *with the negative prefixed.*

منيوش listen not, *the negative imperative of* نيوشيدن

موج A. a wave.

موجب A. a cause; an acceptor.

موزون A. melodious; adjusted, arranged, weighed.

موسم A. time, season.

موصل A. Mawsil, *name of a place.*

موي hair.

موید A. firm.

مهجور A. separated, repudiated. abandoned.

مهر the sun; moon; love; a seal-ring: a gold coin about 1*l.* 16*s.*

مهوش like the moon.

مي wine.

مي *characteristic of the present tense.*

میار do not bring, *the negative imperative of* آوردن

میان between, among: middle.

میامیز do not mix *or* sprinkle, *the negative imperative of* آمیختن

مي بیني thou sawest, *second person present of* دیدن

میخواره a wine drinker; an earthern drinking vessel.

میداني thou knowest.

میر dying, *from* مردن

میرزا the son of a prince *or* great man, a knight. میرزامهدي Mīrzā Mahadī, *proper name.*

میرویي dost thou grow? *from* رستن

میزني thou strikest.

میزیبد is it becoming?

میغ a cloud, a fog.

میفروش a seller of wine, *comp of* مي wine, *and part. of* فروختن

میکشي thou drawest, bearest.

مینالم I complain, *from* نالیدن

میوها fruits.

ن

نا not. نا امید hopeless.

ناب pure, sincere; like.

ناتمام imperfect.

ناچیز worthless, despicable.

نادره A. memorable events; rare.

نادر شاه Nādir Shāh, *proper name*.

ناز blandishments; wantonness.

نازك gentle, tender, delicate.

نازنين elegant, delicate, amiable.

ناشگفته unblown, unblemished.

ناشناس ignorant.

ناصر A. a conqueror, defender.

ناظر A. a spectator, superintendant.

نافه a bag (of musk): the navel.

ناك full of.

ناگه suddenly.

ناگهان unexpectedly.

نالان plaintive, complaining.

ناليدن to complain.

نام a name. نامترا thy name.

نامدار illustrious; a hero.

نامه a book, history.

نان bread.

نايب A. a viceroy, deputy.

نبرد a battle, war.

نبود is not. نبودمي I would not have been.

نبي A. a prophet.

نتابم I will not turn.

نترسي do you not fear.

نتوان it is impossible.

نثار A. scattering, dispersing.

نثر A. prose; to diffuse, strew.

نجستمي I would not have sought, *or* leaped.

نجم A. a star, planet: fortune.

نحو A. grammar, syntax.

نخچير hunting; the chase; prey.

نخست first.

نخشبي Nakshabī, *proper name*.

نر male.

نرگس a narcissus.

نرم gentle, tame; light: soft.

نزد near.

نزل A. descending; hospitality.

نزول A. descent; happening.

نسخي A. Niṣkhī (a transcript) *the character in which* Arabic *manuscripts are generally written.*

نسيم A. a gale.

نشاستن to cause to sit down.

نشاط A. alacrity, pleasure.

نشاندن to fix.

نشستن to sit down.

نشنوي you do not hear.

نشين sitting, *from* نشستن

نصيحت A. counsel, exhortation.

نظامي Nažāmī, *name of a poet.*

نظر A. the sight, the eye.

نظرباز rolling the eyes, ogling.

نظم A. verse; a string of pearls.

نعره زدن to call *or* sing aloud.

نعمت A. a benefit; victuals.

نغز beautiful, good; swift.

نغمت A. music, harmony.

نفس A. soul, self; breath; desire.

نفع A. gain, utility.

نقد A. ready money.

نقش A. painting, embroidery.

نقل A. a narration, report, copy, translation.

نگار a picture, ornament; a beautiful woman.

نگارستان Nagāriṣṭān (a gallery of pictures) *title of a celebrated book.*

نکته subtilties, mysteries.

نگرستن to view.

نکوي *or* نکو good.

نگه *or* نگاه custody, care, observation.

نگه دار preserve thou, *imperat. of* نگه داشتن

نما showing. نمودند they show.

نمودن to show.

نوا melody, voice; wealth.

نواب (*pl. of* نايب) viceroys, &c.

نواختن to soothe.

نواز soothing, *from the above.*

نوازش (*pl.* نوازشات) a favour.

نوازنده soothing, warbling, *from* نواختن

نواله a benefit.

نوبت A. a turn, change, watch. centinal. نوبت زدن to relieve guard.

نوبهار the spring, the early spring; new year.

نوح A. the prophet Noah.

نوحت A. a complaint.

نود ninety.

نور A. light, brightness.

نوروز the first day of spring.

نوزده nineteen.

نوش drinking, a drinker; any thing drinkable, *from* نوشیدن

نوشت *or* نوشتن to write.

نویس write thou, *from the above.*

نه nine.

نه placing, *from*

نهادن to place.

نهاده ایم we have placed.

نهال a tree, shrub.

نهان hidden, *from* نهفتن

نهر A. a river; flowing.

نهفتن to hide, lie hid.

ني a pipe, flute.

نیز even, also: again.

نیست there is not.

نیشتن to write.

نیک good, excellent.

نکو bright, beautiful, elegant.

نیکویي reputation, goodness.

نیل the river Nile.

و

و and; he, she, it.

واپس after, behind, again.

واپس داشتن to detain.

واضح A. evident.

واقعات A. actions, occurrences, events: battles: misfortunes.

وان Vān, or Wān, *name of a town.*

وجود A. essence, substance, existence, nature, body, person.

وجود گرفتن to commit, perform, give a being to.

وار *or* ور like, possessing.

ورق A. a leaf *of a* tree *or* paper.

وز and from.

وزید it blows, *from* وزیدن

وست he, she, it is.

وش like, resembling.

وصال A. enjoyment; arrival; meeting; conjunction.

وضع A. situation: action; gesture.

وفا A. good faith; a promise.

ولي A. but: a prince: a slave.

وي he, she, it; his, her, its.

ويرانه a desert; depopulated.

ه

هایل A. dreadful, terrible.

هجر *or* هجران A. separation, absence.

هجوم A. an assault; impetuosity.

هر *or* هران every: soever.

هرات Harāt, *name of a city.*

هرجاکه whenever.

هرچه *or* هرانچه whatsoever.

هرچندکه *or* هرچند although.

هرکجا wherever.

هرکجاکه wheresoever.

هرگز ever.

هرگزنه never.

هرکه *or* هرانکه whosoever.

هزار a thousand; a nightingale.

هستن to be, exist.

هشت eight. هشتاد eighty.

هشده eighteen.

هفت seven. هفتاد seventy.

هفده seventeen.

هل A. whether, but.

هم and, also; together: both.

هم A. (*annexed to words*) their.

همآشیان of the same nest.

همان only.

هماندم directly.

همآهنگ of the same inclination.

همبزم of the same banquet.

همبستر lying on the same pillow.

همچنین in the same way.

همچون *or* همچو like, as.

همخوابه sleeping together.

همدم breathing together.

همراز an intimate friend.

همنشین sitting together; a companion.

همه all, universal.

همیرسید it arrives, comes.

همیرفتم I went, *from* رفتن

همیشه always.

هندو black; an Indian.

هنگام time, season.

هنوز yet.

هوا A. air: wind: sound.

هیچ no, never.

هیچ میدانی dost thou not know? *from* هیچ دانستن

هیشتن to lay down.

ي

يا O! or.

یاب *or* یابان finding.

یابم I may find, *both from* یافتن

یاد remember: memory, record.

یار a friend, mistress; defender; power, advantage.

یارب O heaven! O Lord! *comp. of* یا O! *and* ربّ a lord, master.

یازده eleven.

یاسمین jessamine.

یافت he found, *from* یافتن to find.

یاقوت a ruby.

یت (*annexed to words*) thy.

ید A. the hand; aid, power, strength.

یش (*annexed to words*) their.

یعني that is to say, viz.

یغما prey, spoil, booty.

یک one.

یکانه a hero, conqueror; incomparable; unequalled.

یکتاي precious, valuable, rare.

یکدانه inestimable, rare.

یکدم one moment.

یکدو one *or* two, a few.

یکدیگر one another.

یکروز one day.

یم (*annexed to words*) my.

یمن Yemen, *Arabia the happy*.

یوسف Joseph.

THE END.